NATIONAL
GEOGRAPHIC

National Parks Cookbook

Death Valley's Spinach Salad With Prickly Pear Vinaigrette (page 80). Opposite: Mount Rainier National Park

NINA ELDER | MELISSA KNIFIC

RECIPE PHOTOGRAPHY BY SCOTT SUCHMAN

National Parks
Cookbook

DISHES INSPIRED BY
AMERICA'S GREAT OUTDOORS

NATIONAL GEOGRAPHIC

WASHINGTON, D.C.

Contents

Page 94

Page 96

It All Started With Yellowstone

On March 1, 1872, the Yellowstone National Park Protection Act was signed into law by President Ulysses S. Grant, creating the first national park in the country, if not the world. That declaration protected more than two million acres in Wyoming, Montana, and eventually Idaho, "for the benefit and enjoyment of the people," a phrase you'll see etched in Yellowstone National Park's Roosevelt Arch as you drive under it.

More than 150 years later, there are now 63 national parks across the country dedicated to the American tradition of protecting and preserving huge swaths of land for exploration, education, and relaxation. When you visit a national park, you might hike or bike, enjoy a scenic drive, or spend time exploring the visitors center. But one thing is for sure: At some point, you're going to need to eat. That's where this book comes in.

Celebrating local and regional foods has always been a big part of the national parks experience. In the early days of the parks, food and lodging were mainly provided by private concessionaires (and that's still sometimes the case today). Railroad companies were instrumental in creating some of the first in-park facilities. In Yellowstone National Park, for example, the Old Faithful Inn was built by the Northern Pacific Railway between 1903 and 1904. Made using local logs and stone, the iconic lodge inspired the architectural style known as parkitecture, where in-park buildings are designed to blend in with the surrounding landscape.

If you were dining at the Old Faithful Inn in the early to mid-1900s, you could expect to enjoy cereal, shirred eggs, and bacon for breakfast and deviled beef ribs and hot or jellied bouillon for lunch. Another example is the Ahwahnee, which opened in California's Yosemite National Park in 1927 and set the gold standard for park lodging and dining, offering visitors gourmet fare with remarkable views.

Over the years, dining options changed as tastes shifted, more parks were added, and

Opposite, clockwise from top left: Zion National Park; Fried Green Tomatoes (page 178); hiking in Olympic National Park; Spruce-Cured Salmon (page 148)

paved roads and cars made the national parks experience a more independent adventure. Visitors could go where they wanted when they wanted—and bring or make their own food, too, such as our Ham & Peach Jam Sandwiches (page 48), which can be made ahead and stashed in a cooler for later.

As we pulled recipes together for this book, we aimed to include a range of cuisines and foods that reflect different aspects of the parks—flora and fauna, culture, tradition, and more. To do that, we researched the history of each park, perused lodge menus past and present, talked to people and chefs who live nearby, and paid attention to the locally grown foods.

Our goal was to create a collection of recipes that highlights the diversity of these unique places that cover glaciers and deserts, ocean reefs and rocky mountains. Some of the dishes have a very direct tie to their associated park, such as the

must-order popovers (page 26) served at Jordan Pond House in Maine's Acadia National Park or the Elk Bolognese (page 110) served at Grand Canyon National Park's El Tovar Hotel in Arizona. Others speak to the place more broadly, whether that's the Ranch Rib Eyes (page 164), inspired by the cattle that were raised in the 1940s in the area that became California's Lassen Volcanic National Park, or the Smoky S'mores Snack Mix (page 105), which you might want to munch on while hiking in Montana's Glacier National Park.

For other recipes, we looked outside the parks to see what nearby restaurants serve hungry visitors. While there are no restaurants in California's Joshua Tree National Park, you might stop in nearby Pioneertown, where we'd suggest trying the delicious tri-tip sandwich at Pappy & Harriet's—or make your own version at home (page 144).

We were also inspired by ingredients that can be found in and near the parklands. You can find six species of huckleberries in Montana's Glacier National Park, and the sweet-tart fruit is great paired with iced tea and lemonade in a Huckleberry Arnold Palmer (page 102). Sir Lancelot

Left: Elk Bolognese (page 110). Right: Jordan Pond House Popovers (page 26). Opposite: The Ahwahnee lodge, Yosemite National Park

Garfield Jones and his family owned the land that is now Florida's Biscayne National Park and became one of the state's top pineapple producers. The Spicy Pineapple Salsa (page 47) is in his honor. And we paid homage to Theodore Roosevelt, the "conservation president," in his namesake park in North Dakota with Bison Osso Buco (page 212), one of the most popular dishes at Theodore's Dining Room.

As we gathered these recipes, themes began to emerge. There was an abundance of hearty food (chili, burgers, stews), a good amount of fish (salmon, lobster, cod, walleye), and more bison than you might imagine, thanks to the role the animal has played in American history. With the number of national parks near the southern border, Mexican-inspired flavors popped up frequently. Start your day with Shortcut Chilaquiles (California's Channel Islands National Park, page 64), have a Sonoran Hot Dog with Ensalada de Nopales (Arizona's Saguaro National Park, pages 202 and 200) for lunch, and end the day with Entomatadas de Pollo (Texas's Big Bend National Park, page 40).

Of course, before there were national parks boundaries, these lands were the homes of Indigenous peoples. We are honored to include recipes from and inspired by these Indigenous traditions, including Grilled Bison Skewers With Wojape (page 38) and Salad of Griddled Squash, Apples, Wild Greens & Toasted Walnuts With Maple Dressing (page 39) from Indigenous chef and South Dakota native Sean Sherman, as well as Fai'ai I'a (page 30) from Samoan chef Muagututia Tuala-Tamaalelagi.

Although the natural wonder of the national parks is best enjoyed in person, you can get a taste of these magnificent landscapes in your home kitchen. Our hope is that as you cook these recipes, you'll learn about the history and significance of these uniquely American places—and maybe plan a national park adventure of your own.

PACIFIC OCEAN

National Park of
American Samoa

Olympic
N.P.

North
Cascades N.P.

WASHINGTON

Mt. Rainier N.P.

Glacier
N.P.

CANADA

MONTANA

Theodore
Roosevelt N.P.

OREGON

IDAHO

Crater Lake N.P.

Yellowstone N.P.

Grand Teton N.P.

Badlands
N.P.

Redwood National
and State Parks

Wind Cave
N.P.

WYOMING

Lassen Volcanic
N.P.

CALIFORNIA

NEVADA

UTAH

Rocky Mountain
N.P.

Great Basin N.P.

Canyonlands
N.P.

Arches N.P.

COLORADO

PACIFIC

OCEAN

Yosemite N.P.

Capitol Reef N.P.

Black Canyon of the
Gunnison N.P.

Pinnacles N.P.

Bryce Canyon N.P.

Sequoia & Kings Canyon N.P.s

Zion N.P.

Great Sand Dunes
N.P. & Pres.

Death Valley
N.P.

Mesa Verde
N.P.

Channel Islands N.P.

Grand
Canyon
N.P.

Petrified
Forest
N.P.

Joshua Tree
N.P.

ARIZONA

NEW MEXICO

White Sands
N.P.

Saguaro N.P.

Carlsbad Caverns
N.P.

MEXICO

Guadalupe Mts.
N.P.

ARCTIC OCEAN

THE
NATIONAL PARKS
OF THE
UNITED STATES

Gates of the Arctic
N.P. & Preserve

Kobuk Valley N.P.

CANADA

ALASKA

Big Bend
N.P.

Denali N.P. & Pres.

Wrangell-St. Elias
N.P. & Preserve

Lake Clark N.P. & Pres.

Kenai Fjords
N.P.

Glacier Bay
N.P. & Pres.

Katmai N.P. & Pres.

PACIFIC OCEAN

Voyageurs N.P.

Isle Royale N.P.

Acadia N.P.

Indiana Dunes N.P.

Cuyahoga Valley N.P.

Shenandoah N.P.

New River Gorge N.P. & Preserve

Gateway Arch N.P.

Mammoth Cave N.P.

Great Smoky Mts. N.P.

Hot Springs N.P.

Congaree N.P.

Biscayne N.P.

Everglades N.P.

Dry Tortugas N.P.

Haleakalā N.P.

Hawai'i Volcanoes N.P.

Virgin Islands N.P.

Denali National Park & Preserve

The bus ride is well worth the effort to spend a day amid the berry bushes in the fields surrounding 649-acre Wonder Lake in Alaska's Denali National Park and Preserve.

Joshua Tree National Park

After a day of hiking in California's high desert, bring your appetite to Pappy & Harriet's. The restaurant, which was founded in 1982, is known for its Santa Maria–style barbecue and Wild West aesthetic.

Glacier
National Park

Lights from the historic Many Glacier Hotel, built in 1915 in the style of a Swiss chalet, reflect off the waters of Swiftcurrent Lake in Montana's Glacier National Park.

Everglades National Park

Founder and owner Robert Moehling works the counter at bustling Robert Is Here Fruit Stand and Farm, which has served the community surrounding the Florida park for more than 60 years.

Capitol Reef National Park

Utah's Fruita Historic District is home to an orchard boasting a variety of fruits including cherries, pears, apples, and plums. It's also the site of the only developed campground within the park.

Grand Teton
National Park

Every table in the Mural Room of Jackson Lake Lodge in Wyoming's Grand Teton National Park has an expansive view of the Teton Range and Jackson Lake.

ACADIA NATIONAL PARK

Lobster Stew

Lobster is a quintessential Maine food, and given Acadia's 64 miles of coastline, getting your fill of it on a visit to the park is a no-brainer. You can order a Maine lobster roll at Acadia's Jordan Pond House, the last remaining teahouse on Mount Desert Island in the heart of the park, or you can go in a cozier direction and opt for a bowl of the lobster stew. The tender chunks of lobster are served in a rich, creamy broth with a hint of sherry.

YIELD: 4 TO 6 SERVINGS
HANDS-ON TIME: 20 MINUTES
TOTAL TIME: 20 MINUTES

3 tablespoons unsalted butter

1 cup (8 ounces) chopped raw or cooked lobster meat

¼ teaspoon paprika

3 cups milk

1 cup light cream

1 tablespoon lobster stock concentrate (sometimes labeled lobster base)

Salt and white pepper

1 tablespoon dry sherry

Vermont Common Crackers or oyster crackers

Chopped fresh chives

1. In a medium skillet, melt butter over low heat. Add lobster meat and paprika. If using raw lobster, cook, stirring occasionally, until meat is tender and cooked through, about 10 minutes. (If using cooked lobster, warm, stirring occasionally, until meat is heated through, about 5 minutes.)

2. Meanwhile, in a medium pot, whisk together milk, cream, and lobster concentrate until combined. Cook over medium heat, stirring occasionally, until steaming, about 5 minutes.

3. Add lobster to milk mixture, and stir to combine. Season with salt and white pepper to taste, and stir in sherry.

4. Serve with Vermont Common Crackers (split and toasted) or oyster crackers and chives.

Monument Cove

Jordan Pond House Popovers

Dining on warm popovers with local Maine jam has been a tradition at Acadia's Jordan Pond House since the 1890s, when Nellie McIntire, the first proprietor of the restaurant, started making and serving the puffy pastries. The same recipe is used today, though it's been scaled up a bit since close to 3,500 popovers are served during the peak summer season (that's 42 five-gallon buckets of batter every day!). Although you can enjoy these treasured treats—offered with tea or prosecco or served as part of a dessert sundae—inside, the pro move is to snag a table on the lawn and enjoy yours with a view of the pond.

YIELD: 6 FULL-SIZE OR
8 MUFFIN-SIZE POPOVERS
HANDS-ON TIME: 25 MINUTES
TOTAL TIME: 55 MINUTES

1 cup (120 grams) sifted all-purpose flour

½ teaspoon kosher salt or ¼ teaspoon fine sea salt

¼ teaspoon baking soda

Butter, for greasing pan and serving

2 large eggs

1 cup (240 ml) whole milk, divided

Jam (optional)

1. Preheat oven to 425°F. In a medium bowl, mix flour, salt, and baking soda until combined. Generously grease a popover pan or muffin pan with butter.

Ranger and Boys Looking Westward in Acadia National Park, Bar Harbor, Mt. Desert Island, Maine

2. Using an electric mixer, beat eggs in a large bowl on high speed until lemon-colored, 2 to 3 minutes.

3. Reduce speed to low, and gradually add ½ cup milk, beating until well blended. Gradually add dry ingredients, beating until just blended, about 2 minutes.

4. Scrape sides of bowl, increase speed to medium, and gradually add remaining ½ cup milk; beat for 2 minutes. Increase speed to high, and beat until batter is smooth and roughly the consistency of heavy cream, 5 to 7 minutes.

5. If using a popover pan, pour ½ cup batter into each well. If using a muffin pan, pour batter into each well so each is about ⅔ full.

6. Bake popovers for 15 minutes, then reduce heat to 350°F (do not open the oven). Bake until popovers are golden brown and fully puffed, 15 to 20 minutes.

7. Serve warm with butter and jam, if desired.

Acadia
National Park

Acadia's rugged coastline and stunning views have attracted sightseers to Maine for generations. The park encompasses roughly 50,000 acres along the eastern seaboard.

Fai'ai I'a

Most national park lands are federally owned, but the National Park of American Samoa is different. The three remote islands that make up the park are leased from local villages in respect for the Samoan culture, which is at the forefront of the park. While visitors can walk through tropical rainforests, snorkel in coral reefs, and discover secluded villages, food is also deeply rooted in the local environment. Coconut, seafood, and taro—staples in Samoan cuisine—are showcased in this classic dish from Muagututia Tuala-Tamaalelagi, the Samoan chef-owner of Fresh Off Da Boat in Sacramento, California.

YIELD: 4 SERVINGS
HANDS-ON TIME: 30 MINUTES
TOTAL TIME: 1 HOUR, INCLUDING STANDING

2 tablespoons unsalted butter

¼ cup thinly sliced yellow onion

1 teaspoon finely chopped garlic

Pinch of crushed red pepper

1 (13.5-ounce) can unsweetened coconut cream

¼ cup dry white wine

1 medium green plantain, cut into bite-size (½- to ¾-inch) pieces (about 1 cup)

1 small taro root, cut into bite-size pieces (about 1 cup; see note)

¼ cup braised taro leaves (or cooked spinach or kale)

¼ cup halved cherry tomatoes

Salt and pepper

1 pound mullet or any white fish, such as halibut

1 lemon

1. Preheat oven to 375°F. Melt butter in a medium cast-iron or heavy oven-proof skillet over medium heat. Add onion, garlic, and crushed red pepper. Cook, stirring often, until onion is translucent, about 5 minutes.

2. Pour coconut cream and wine into skillet, stirring and scraping bottom of skillet. Bring mixture to a simmer, then stir in plantain, taro root, taro leaves, and tomatoes. Season with salt and pepper. Let simmer until sauce is reduced by a little more than half, about 5 minutes.

3. Add fish to skillet, submerging in sauce. Season with salt and pepper.

4. Transfer skillet to oven, and bake until fish is flaky and top is golden brown, 15 to 20 minutes. Remove from oven, and squeeze juice from half of lemon over fish. Let stand for 15 minutes before serving with remaining lemon half, cut into wedges.

Recipe Note

Taro is likely one of the oldest known food plants in the world, but take care when preparing it, as the roots and leaves are poisonous when raw. Cooking will neutralize them.

Delicate Arch

Graham Cracker Milkshake

Regular visitors to Arches National Park know that the best place to head after a hike is Milt's Stop & Eat. Milt Galbraith opened the restaurant in 1954 (the website claims it's the oldest restaurant in Moab, Utah). Galbraith passed away in 2014, but Milt's Stop & Eat has remained largely unchanged. Hungry hikers can pop in for a burger, made with local, grass-fed beef, and wash it down with a shake, like this one.

YIELD: 1 MILKSHAKE
HANDS-ON TIME: 10 MINUTES
TOTAL TIME: 10 MINUTES

2 cups vanilla ice cream

½ cup graham cracker crumbs, plus more for topping

1 tablespoon milk

½ teaspoon granulated sugar

½ teaspoon ground cinnamon

For serving: whipped cream, chocolate syrup, maraschino cherry

1. Combine ice cream, graham cracker crumbs, milk, sugar, and cinnamon in a blender. Process until smooth. Pour into a tall, chilled glass. Top with whipped cream, chocolate syrup, a cherry, and more graham cracker crumbs.

33

No-Bake Apricot-Almond Granola Bars

There are more than 2,000 natural stone arches in Utah's aptly named Arches National Park, along with hundreds of pinnacles and teetering rock towers. The geology of this red rock wonderland makes hiking one of the park's main draws, with trails ranging from a few hundred yards to more than seven miles. No matter the route, every hiker needs some fuel for the trail, and these no-bake granola bars are a simple, hearty snack to put in your pack. Paying homage to the park, the apricots and almonds are an ode to the nearby orchards, but feel free to customize this recipe with any dried fruits and nuts.

YIELD: 12 BARS
HANDS-ON TIME: 15 MINUTES
TOTAL TIME: 2 HOURS 15 MINUTES, INCLUDING CHILLING

3 cups old-fashioned rolled oats

1 cup dried apricots, chopped

⅔ cup sliced almonds, toasted

1 teaspoon ground cinnamon

½ teaspoon kosher salt

1 cup unsweetened smooth almond butter

⅔ cup honey

½ teaspoon vanilla extract or ¼ teaspoon almond extract

Flaky salt (optional)

Turret Arch

1. Line the bottom and sides of an 8-inch-square pan with parchment paper, letting parchment hang 1 to 2 inches over the sides for easy removal. Coat with nonstick cooking spray.

2. In a large bowl, combine oats, apricots, almonds, cinnamon, and kosher salt until well blended.

3. In a small bowl, mix together almond butter, honey, and vanilla until smooth. Add almond butter mixture to oat mixture, stirring with a silicone spatula until oat mixture is well coated.

4. Transfer mixture to prepared pan, and use the spatula and your fingers to very firmly press mixture to the edges, creating a smooth, even, dense layer. (Grease your hands to help prevent sticking.) Sprinkle with flaky salt, if using. Cover tightly with plastic wrap, and refrigerate until firm (at least 2 hours).

5. Once firm, remove from pan, using the parchment. Cut into 12 bars with a sharp knife, wiping the blade in between slices if necessary. Store in an airtight container in the refrigerator for up to a week. (The bars can also be frozen: Place them on a sheet pan with space between each, and freeze. Transfer to a zip-top plastic bag, and store in freezer up to 3 months.)

Salad of Griddled Squash, Apples, Wild Greens & Toasted Walnuts With Maple Dressing (page 39) and Grilled Bison Skewers With Wojape (page 38)

Grilled Bison Skewers With Wojape

Recipe adapted with permission from *The Sioux Chef's Indigenous Kitchen* by Sean Sherman with Beth Dooley

There's evidence of humans in the area in and around what's now South Dakota's Badlands National Park dating back 12,000 years. Archaeologists believe the land was a seasonal hunting area for Indigenous people. Sean Sherman—chef, cookbook author, and founder of the Indigenous Food Lab—is a member of the Oglala Lakota Sioux tribe and grew up not far from the park. He has made it his mission to revitalize Indigenous food systems—and to build awareness around Native foods. This recipe from his cookbook showcases several ingredients you can find in and around Badlands, including bison, chokecherries, and turnips.

YIELD: 4 TO 6 SERVINGS
HANDS-ON TIME: 35 MINUTES
TOTAL TIME: 35 MINUTES

WOJAPE

6 cups fresh chokecherries (or an assortment of blueberries, raspberries, strawberries, elderberries, cranberries, or blackberries)

1 to 1½ cups water

Honey or maple syrup, to taste

BISON SKEWERS

1 to 1½ pounds bison sirloin, cut into 1- to 2-inch cubes

2 tablespoons sunflower oil

Ground sumac

Smoked salt

2 or 3 ears sweet corn, shucked and cut into 2-inch chunks

2 to 4 small turnips, cut into 2-inch chunks

3 yellow squash, cut into 2-inch chunks

1. To make the wojape, put berries and 1 to 1½ cups water into a saucepan over low heat. Bring to a simmer, and cook, stirring occasionally, until mixture is thick. Taste and season with honey or maple syrup as desired.

2. To make the bison skewers, preheat a gas or charcoal grill to medium-high (350°F to 400°F) heat.

3. Brush bison with 1 tablespoon sunflower oil, and sprinkle with a pinch of sumac and smoked salt. Brush corn, turnips, and squash with remaining 1 tablespoon sunflower oil.

4. Thread bison, corn, turnips, and squash alternately on 4 to 6 skewers. Sprinkle with a pinch of sumac and smoked salt.

5. Grill skewers, covered with grill lid and turning frequently, until bison is no longer pink in center, 15 to 20 minutes. Remove skewers from grill, and drizzle with wojape.

Salad of Griddled Squash, Apples, Wild Greens & Toasted Walnuts With Maple Dressing

Recipe adapted with permission from *The Sioux Chef's Indigenous Kitchen* by Sean Sherman with Beth Dooley

Sean Sherman, a member of the Oglala Lakota Sioux tribe, didn't eat a lot of Indigenous foods while he was growing up near Badlands National Park. Today, that has all changed. The chef and cookbook author has dedicated his career to showcasing and sharing traditional Native American foodways, including those from his home state of South Dakota, like this salad of wild greens, squash, apples, and nuts. It pairs very well with his Grilled Bison Skewers With Wojape (at left).

YIELD: 4 TO 6 SERVINGS
HANDS-ON TIME: 25 MINUTES
TOTAL TIME: 25 MINUTES

MAPLE DRESSING

⅓ cup sunflower oil

¼ cup apple cider vinegar

2 tablespoons maple syrup, or more to taste

1 teaspoon ground mustard

Salt

SALAD

1 small acorn or delicata squash, peeled, seeded, and diced

1 medium or 2 small apples, cored, peeled, and sliced or diced

2 tablespoons sunflower oil

6 to 8 cups mixed wild greens

¼ cup dried cranberries

1 teaspoon chopped fresh sage

¼ cup maple dressing (above), plus more for for drizzling

¼ cup toasted, chopped walnuts

1. To make the maple dressing, place the oil, vinegar, 2 tablespoons maple syrup, and ground mustard in a small jar and shake vigorously. Season to taste with salt and more maple syrup.

2. To make the salad, brush squash and apple with oil.

3. Heat a skillet over medium-high heat, and add squash, cooking until browned and tender on both sides, about 5 to 10 minutes per side. Remove from skillet. Toast apple in skillet until slightly browned, about 2 to 4 minutes.

4. In a large bowl, toss greens, cranberries, and sage with dressing, and arrange on a serving platter or individual plates.

5. Arrange squash and apple over greens, and drizzle with more dressing, as desired. Top with walnuts.

Entomatadas de Pollo

Big Bend National Park in West Texas shares a 118-mile-long border with Mexico along the Rio Grande, so it makes sense that areas surrounding the U.S. national park have adopted much of its neighboring country's cuisine. A cousin to enchiladas, these *entomatadas* are lightly fried, stuffed with chicken and cheese, and draped in a tomatoey sauce. Top them as you like, but don't forget a side of Frijoles Refritos (page 42).

YIELD: 4 SERVINGS
HANDS-ON TIME: 30 MINUTES
TOTAL TIME: 1 HOUR

1 large white onion

1 pound medium tomatoes

1 serrano or jalapeño pepper

4 large cloves garlic

1 tablespoon vegetable oil, plus more for frying

½ cup fresh cilantro leaves and tender stems, roughly chopped, plus more for serving

¼ teaspoon ground cumin

1¼ cups water

Salt

12 (6-inch) corn tortillas

4 cups shredded cooked chicken, warmed

8 ounces queso fresco, crumbled

For serving: crema or sour cream, cotija cheese, diced onion, cilantro, and lime wedges (optional)

1. Arrange oven rack in position closest to the heat source; preheat broiler. Halve onion; slice one half into ½-inch wedges, and dice remaining half.

2. Line a baking sheet with aluminum foil; arrange onion wedges, tomatoes, serrano, and garlic on baking sheet. Broil until mixture is charred, 10 to 12 minutes, turning tomatoes and pepper halfway through. Remove from oven, and allow tomatoes to cool slightly, then peel and discard skins.

3. Put onion wedges, tomatoes, serrano, and garlic in a blender or food processor. Pulse until slightly chunky.

4. Heat 1 tablespoon oil in a large saucepan over medium-high heat. Carefully pour in tomato mixture, and bring to a simmer (be mindful of splattering). Cook, stirring frequently, over medium-high heat until sauce has darkened and thickened almost like tomato paste, 6 to 7 minutes. Stir in cilantro, cumin, and 1¼ cups water. Bring to a boil, reduce heat to medium, and simmer until reduced and slightly thickened, 12 to 15 minutes. Season with salt, remove from heat, and cover to keep warm.

5. In a medium skillet, heat ½ inch of oil over medium-high heat until shimmering. Fry 1 tortilla until very lightly browned, 5 to 10 seconds per side. Using tongs, dip fried tortilla into the warm tomato sauce, turning to coat, then transfer to a serving plate. Fill tortilla with chicken and queso fresco, then fold in half over the filling. Repeat until all tortillas have been fried, dipped, and filled.

6. Bring remaining tomato sauce to a simmer over medium-high heat, and spoon it evenly over tortillas. Serve immediately, topped with crema, cotija, diced onion, and cilantro, as desired. Serve with lime wedges, if using.

Santa Elena Canyon and the Rio Grande

Frijoles Refritos

You're guaranteed to find *frijoles refritos*, or refried beans, on dozens of menus in restaurants surrounding Texas's Big Bend National Park. The hearty side dish is packed with protein to help you hike all day in the Chihuahuan Desert and sparse Chisos Mountains. Although you can make refried beans with canned beans, using dried beans creates a depth of flavor canned can't touch.

YIELD: 4 TO 6 SERVINGS
HANDS-ON TIME: 30 MINUTES
TOTAL TIME: 2 HOURS 30 MINUTES

1 medium white onion

1 pound dried pinto beans

4 large cloves garlic

3 fresh oregano or epazote sprigs

1 tablespoon kosher salt, plus more to taste

2 tablespoons bacon drippings, lard, or vegetable oil

Crumbled cotija, fresh cilantro leaves, and lime wedges

1. Halve onion; quarter one half, and dice remaining half. Rinse and sort beans, and add to a large Dutch oven or heavy-bottomed pot with quartered onion, garlic, oregano, salt, and water to cover by 3 inches. Stir to combine.

2. Bring to a boil over medium-high heat. Reduce heat to medium-low and partially cover. Simmer, stirring occasionally, until beans are very tender, 2 to 2½ hours (they'll easily break apart when gently squeezed between a thumb and forefinger). Drain beans, reserving liquid in pot. Discard oregano stems and any large pieces of onion.

3. In a large skillet, melt bacon drippings over medium-high heat. Add drained bean mixture. Fry, stirring often, for 2 minutes. Add ½ cup reserved bean liquid. Using a potato masher or back of a spoon, smash to desired consistency, adding more bean liquid if desired. Turn off heat, and season with salt. (Beans can take a lot of salt, so don't be shy!)

4. Top beans with diced onion, cotija, and cilantro. Serve with lime wedges.

Texas sage blooms in Big Bend.

Recipe Note

If desired, you can save the remaining bean liquid in a separate container, then add some to the leftover beans when reheating. To reheat: Heat 2 tablespoons oil in a skillet, add leftover beans and a bit of the reserved bean liquid, and cook, stirring, until hot.

*Grilled Whole Red Snapper (page 46)
and Spicy Pineapple Salsa (page 47)*

Grilled Whole Red Snapper

One of the best ways to experience the beauty of Biscayne's coral reefs, mangroves, and islands is by boat—and docking and dining is a thing around the Florida marine park. Several restaurants in Miami, to the north of the park, cater to hungry boaters looking to grab a bite after a long day on the water. Grilled whole red snapper, a fish common to Biscayne Bay, frequently appears on menus. This simple preparation—with Key limes, if you can find them—lets the fish shine.

YIELD: 4 SERVINGS
HANDS-ON TIME: 25 MINUTES
TOTAL TIME: 35 MINUTES

3 to 4 Key or regular limes, divided

2 whole red snapper (1½ to 2 pounds each), cleaned and scaled (see note)

Olive oil, for brushing and drizzling

Salt and pepper

1 bunch fresh cilantro

Spicy Pineapple Salsa (at right), for serving (optional)

Recipe Note
Ask your grocer's fishmonger to clean and scale the fish for you.

1. Preheat grill to high heat (400°F to 450°F). Zest 2 limes, then thinly slice both into rounds.

2. Pat both fish dry inside and out with paper towels. Using a sharp paring knife, cut three ¼-inch-deep diagonal slits on both sides of each fish.

3. Drizzle olive oil inside fish cavities, and generously season with salt and pepper. Layer lime slices and a handful of cilantro sprigs inside cavities. Generously brush outsides of fish with olive oil (this will prevent it from sticking to the grill). Rub with lime zest, and season generously with salt and pepper, making sure seasonings get inside the slits.

4. Grill fish, covered with grill lid, until flesh is firm and flaky and outside skin has char marks, 5 to 7 minutes per side.

5. Transfer fish to a platter. Cut remaining limes into wedges. Drizzle fish with olive oil, and sprinkle with cilantro sprigs. Serve immediately with lime wedges and Spicy Pineapple Salsa, if desired.

Spicy Pineapple Salsa

Americans have Sir Lancelot Garfield Jones to thank for the preserved beauty of Biscayne National Park. Jones was born on a sailboat in Biscayne Bay in 1898 to Israel Lafayette Jones and Mozelle Albury, the first Black landowners in the Florida Keys. Eventually, the family became one of the largest Key lime and pineapple producers in the state. After his parents' deaths, Jones fought to protect their land, ultimately selling it to the U.S. government instead of a corporation. This pineapple salsa is an ode to Jones's tireless conservation work.

YIELD: ABOUT 2 CUPS
HANDS-ON TIME: 15 MINUTES
TOTAL TIME: 15 MINUTES

2 cups diced fresh pineapple (½-inch cubes)

1 small Fresno chile or jalapeño pepper, seeded and minced

1 small shallot, minced

1 lime, zested and halved

½ teaspoon kosher salt

½ cup fresh cilantro, chopped

1. In a medium bowl, toss together pineapple, pepper, shallot, and lime zest. Squeeze juice from lime over mixture, and add salt. Toss until well combined. Stir in cilantro. Serve immediately, or refrigerate for a few hours to allow the flavors to meld.

Ham & Peach Jam Sandwiches

Western Colorado's Black Canyon of the Gunnison National Park is known for its striking geologic features. Over millions of years, the area was lifted, buried in volcanic rock, and then eroded into a deep, dramatic canyon, cut through by the Gunnison River. Visitors can explore the park's scenic drives and many nature trails, where you might be lucky enough to see a peregrine falcon, the world's fastest animal. To fuel all your adventures, pack a lunch. This sandwich is the perfect thing to slip into your backpack or cooler and was inspired by the outstanding peaches that are grown in western Colorado.

DETROIT PHOTOGRAPHIC CO., PUBLISHERS.

6715. CURRECANTI NEEDLE, BLACK CANYON OF THE GUNNISON, COLORADO.

Jamie's—
Went to the State Capitol to day, got a good view of the mountains
E.C.

YIELD: 4 SANDWICHES
HANDS-ON TIME: 15 MINUTES
TOTAL TIME: 25 MINUTES, INCLUDING STANDING

4 sub rolls (6 to 9 inches long), halved lengthwise

1 (4-ounce) log herbed or plain goat cheese

¼ cup peach jam

1 pound deli-sliced ham (plain or Black Forest)

2 cups baby arugula or baby spinach

Olive oil and balsamic vinegar

Salt and pepper

1 large peach, thinly sliced (optional)

1. On bottom half of sub rolls, spread goat cheese (about 1½ tablespoons per sandwich). Top with peach jam and ham.

2. Divide arugula among sandwiches, and drizzle with olive oil and vinegar. Season with desired amount of salt and pepper. Add peach slices, if using, and top halves of rolls.

3. Using parchment or wax paper, tightly wrap each sandwich. Let stand at room temperature 30 minutes. (If you're preparing these more than 30 minutes ahead, transfer sandwiches to the refrigerator for up to 4 hours.) Wrapping helps the sandwiches stay together. The longer the standing time, the more the flavors will meld.

Dutch Oven Potatoes

Travelers head to this park to marvel at the hoodoos (striking rock spires) of the Bryce Canyon Amphitheater, which holds the world's greatest concentration of this geologic feature. If you linger a bit longer, you can also camp under some pretty incredible dark skies. While you're camping, pick up some firewood and try your hand at Dutch oven potatoes, a classic southern Utah dish of cheesy potatoes, onions, and bacon cooked over a live fire. This version comes together in the oven to give you a taste of Utah at home.

YIELD: 12 SERVINGS
HANDS-ON TIME: 30 MINUTES
TOTAL TIME: 1 HOUR 30 MINUTES

1 pound thick-cut smoked bacon, diced

1 large yellow or white onion, diced

4 cloves garlic, chopped

1 tablespoon butter

5 or 6 russet potatoes (4 pounds), very thinly sliced (about ¼-inch thick)

Kosher salt and pepper

3 cups (12 ounces) shredded Colby Jack cheese

1 (4-ounce) can diced mild green chiles

Sliced green onions and hot sauce (optional)

1. Preheat oven to 350°F.

2. Cook bacon in a large Dutch oven or cast-iron pot over medium heat, stirring occasionally, until it starts to release its fat, about 4 minutes. Add onion, and cook until nearly softened, 3 to 4 minutes. Stir in garlic, and cook 1 minute. Transfer to a plate using a slotted spoon.

3. Add butter to pot. Once melted, add one-third of sliced potatoes in an even layer, and sprinkle generously with salt and pepper. Add half of bacon-onion mixture and ¾ cup cheese. Repeat layering with one-third of potatoes sprinkled with salt and pepper, remaining bacon-onion mixture, and ¾ cup cheese. Add remaining one-third of potatoes, and season generously with salt and pepper. Cover pot with lid or tightly with aluminum foil.

4. Bake for 45 minutes. Uncover, and scatter chiles and remaining 1½ cups cheese on top. Cover pot again and bake until potatoes are easily pierced with a fork and cheese is melted, about 15 minutes.

5. Serve potatoes with green onions and hot sauce, if desired.

Recipe Note

To make this heartier, add 1 pound ground beef along with the onion in step 2, and cook until browned and crumbly. Proceed with the recipe as directed.

Bryce Canyon National Park

A pair of horseback riders pause at an over-look circa 1960. Bryce Canyon's hoodoos (irregular columns of rocks) are part of a geologic history that dates back 50 million years.

Juniper-Mint Lemonade

Utah's juniper trees defy the laws of botany, majestically towering above the harsh, rocky landscape of Canyonlands National Park. While the sun can be unbearable during the day, the nighttime brings bone-chilling temperatures. Between those extremes, and near-nothing rainfall and heavy winds, these trees miraculously fight to exist. Every fall, the Utah juniper bears fruit, a tiny berry that's a staple for local wildlife. This thirst-quenching lemonade celebrates these iconic trees and their will to keep on giving.

YIELD: 12 SERVINGS
HANDS-ON TIME: 10 MINUTES
TOTAL TIME: 50 MINUTES, INCLUDING INFUSING

¼ cup dried juniper berries

1 cup granulated sugar

9 cups cold water, divided

1½ cups lemon juice (from 10 to 12 lemons), plus 2 lemons, thinly sliced

Pinch of fine sea salt

Ice and fresh mint sprigs (optional)

1. Crush juniper berries using a mortar and pestle, or by carefully pressing them on a cutting board with the side of a large knife.

2. In a small pot, combine crushed juniper berries, sugar, and 1 cup water. Bring to a boil over high heat. Reduce heat to medium-low, and simmer, stirring frequently, until sugar is dissolved, 2 to 3 minutes. Turn off the heat, and let infuse 30 minutes.

3. Pour syrup through a fine-mesh strainer into a jar or glass measuring cup. Discard berries. Cool completely.

4. Once syrup is cool, add to a large pitcher with lemon juice, salt, and remaining 8 cups cold water. Stir until combined, then add lemon slices.

5. Serve lemonade over ice with mint, if desired. Refrigerate any remaining lemonade, covered, for up to a week.

A lone juniper tree

No-Churn Cinnamon Ice Cream (page 59) and
Mini Apple Crumble Pies (page 58)

Mini Apple Crumble Pies

Within a mile or two of the Capitol Reef National Park Visitor Center in Utah, you'll find orchards—the remnants of a Mormon settlement called Fruita. The small community of about 10 families lived here from the late 1800s to the late 1960s and grew fruit trees, sorghum, vegetables, and alfalfa. Today, about 1,900 trees (cherry, peach, and apple) are managed by the Park Service. Visitors can explore the orchards year-round and can occasionally pick fruit when U-pick signs are posted. Take the fruit home to make your own dessert, or stop by the Gifford Homestead inside the park, where you can pick up a mini pie made with local fruit.

YIELD: 8 (5-INCH) PIES
HANDS-ON TIME: 1 HOUR
TOTAL TIME: 2 HOURS 50 MINUTES, INCLUDING CHILLING

CRUST

3 cups (360 grams) all-purpose flour

1 tablespoon packed brown sugar

1½ teaspoons kosher salt

1¼ cups (2½ sticks) cold unsalted butter, cut into cubes

1 tablespoon apple cider vinegar

¼ cup ice water

CRUMBLE TOPPING

1 cup (120 grams) all-purpose flour

1 cup (100 grams) old-fashioned rolled oats

½ cup (1 stick) unsalted butter, melted

½ cup (112 grams) packed brown sugar

¼ teaspoon kosher salt

FILLING

2¾ to 3 pounds assorted apples (such as Granny Smith and Honeycrisp), cored, peeled, and diced into ½-inch cubes (about 7 cups)

2 tablespoons packed brown sugar

2 tablespoons cornstarch

2 teaspoons fresh lemon juice

½ teaspoon ground cinnamon

¼ teaspoon kosher salt

¼ teaspoon ground cardamom

1. To make the crust, pulse flour, brown sugar, and salt in a food processor until combined. Sprinkle butter cubes over flour, and pulse until largest pieces of butter are the size of peas, about 10 pulses. Drizzle vinegar and 2 tablespoons ice water over mixture, then pulse until dough holds together when pinched, 5 to 10 pulses. If dough is still dry, add remaining ice water by the teaspoonful and pulse.

2. Transfer dough to a work surface. Gather into a ball, then press into a rectangle. Cut dough in half, and place one half on top of the other; press into one piece. Divide dough in half, flatten into two disks, wrap in plastic wrap, and chill until firm, about 1 hour.

3. While dough chills, make crumble topping. Mix together flour, oats, butter, brown sugar, and salt in a medium bowl until oats are coated. Refrigerate for 15 minutes.

4. While dough and topping chill, make the filling. Toss together apples, brown sugar, cornstarch, lemon juice, cinnamon, salt, and cardamom in a large bowl until apples are evenly coated.

5. Arrange oven racks in top and bottom thirds of oven. Preheat oven to 425°F. Roll one dough

Recipe Note

You can use mini pie pans, either aluminum or reusable, for this recipe. If you'd like to make the pies in advance, you can make the dough ahead through step 2, and store it in the refrigerator for 1 day, or freeze for up to 3 months. The baked pies also freeze well. Wrap cooled baked pies tightly in plastic wrap or aluminum foil, place in zip-top plastic bags, and freeze for up to 4 months. To rewarm, uncover and bake from frozen at 375°F until warm.

disk into a 14-inch circle (about ⅜ inch thick) on a work surface. Place 3 (5-inch) mini pie pans upside down on dough, leaving about 1 inch of dough around each. Using a small, sharp knife, cut out 3 rounds of dough (about 6 inches each). Gather scraps, roll to ⅜ inch, and cut out 1 more round.

6. Fit dough rounds into 4 pie pans, pressing on bottom and up sides of pans. Press dough around edges of pans or crimp with your fingers or a fork. Repeat with remaining dough disk.

7. Chill crusts until firm, about 15 minutes. (This will help keep crusts from shrinking in pans.)

8. Divide filling among pie pans (about 1 cup per pie). Top each with crumble topping, dividing equally (about ¼ cup per pie). Place pies on baking sheets to catch any overflow while baking.

9. Bake at 425°F for 10 minutes; reduce heat to 375°F, and bake, alternating racks halfway through baking, until crusts are brown, filling is tender, and crumble topping is lightly browned, about 25 minutes. Cool slightly before serving. Make it à la mode with No-Churn Cinnamon Ice Cream (at right).

No-Churn Cinnamon Ice Cream

Wrinkles are often seen as something to get rid of, whether they're in fabric or on your face. But a wrinkle is the reason that Utah's Capitol Reef National Park is so stunning. Thanks to the Waterpocket Fold, a geologic monocline (aka a wrinkle in the earth), visitors can marvel at winding canyons, graceful arches, layer cake–like cliffs, and domes that reminded settlers of buildings in the nation's capital and inspired the park's name. Among the colorful cliffs, you'll find a green valley and the Gifford Homestead, a former farm that's now run by the Capitol Reef Natural History Association, and whose legacy lives on in the form of homemade ice cream (the inspiration for this recipe) that visitors line up for.

YIELD: 8 SERVINGS
HANDS-ON TIME: 15 MINUTES
TOTAL TIME: 3 HOURS 15 MINUTES, INCLUDING FREEZING

1 (14-ounce) can sweetened condensed milk

4 ounces cream cheese, at room temperature

1 teaspoon ground cinnamon

1 teaspoon vanilla extract

¼ teaspoon kosher salt

1½ cups chilled heavy cream

2 teaspoons packed brown sugar

1. In a large bowl, whisk together sweetened condensed milk, cream cheese, cinnamon, vanilla, and salt until smooth.

2. Place heavy cream in a large bowl. Crumble brown sugar over heavy cream to help prevent lumps. Beat at high speed with an electric mixer until cream holds a medium peak, about 3 minutes.

3. Gently fold the whipped cream into condensed milk mixture until mostly combined (a few whipped cream streaks are fine).

4. Transfer mixture to a loaf pan or small baking dish, smoothing the top. Freeze until solid, about 3 hours. Let stand a few minutes before scooping if ice cream is too hard.

Frito Pie

In the heart of the Southwest lies New Mexico's Carlsbad Caverns National Park, with a desert landscape aboveground and more than 30 miles of limestone caves beneath its surface. Within the park is Carlsbad Caverns Trading Company, where visitors can grab a quick bite, including a regional favorite, Frito Pie. In the dish, a rich beef and bean chili is mounded over corn chips and topped with Hatch green chile salsa verde, another Southwestern staple. While you're at the park, make sure to also check out the Underground Lunchroom, a snack spot that's 750 feet below the visitors center.

YIELD: 6 SERVINGS
HANDS-ON TIME: 15 MINUTES
TOTAL TIME: 1 HOUR

1 tablespoon vegetable oil

1 pound ground beef

2 tablespoons chili powder

1½ teaspoons garlic powder

1½ teaspoons ground cumin

1½ teaspoons paprika

1 teaspoon onion powder

1 teaspoon dried oregano

1 teaspoon kosher salt

½ teaspoon pepper

1 (15.5-ounce) can pinto beans

1 (15.5-ounce) can kidney beans

1 (15.5-ounce) can black beans

1 (14-ounce) can tomato sauce

1 (12-ounce) bag corn chips, such as Fritos

For serving: shredded cheddar cheese, sour cream, shredded lettuce, pickled jalapeño peppers, salsa verde, pico de gallo

1. Heat oil in a large Dutch oven or heavy-bottomed pot over medium-high heat. Add beef, chili powder, garlic powder, cumin, paprika, onion powder, oregano, salt, and pepper. Cook, breaking meat into pieces, until fully cooked and brown, about 5 minutes.

2. Stir in all the beans and their liquid (do not drain) and tomato sauce. Reduce heat to low, cover, and simmer, stirring occasionally, until reduced, 30 minutes. Uncover, and simmer, stirring occasionally, 15 minutes. Season with salt to taste.

3. Fill each bowl with a large handful of corn chips, then ladle chili on top. Serve with desired toppings.

Rock of Ages

Ventura-Style Fish Tacos With Jicama Slaw

Fish tacos likely first popped up in Baja California, Mexico, but the dish soon spread north, up the coast of California. Ventura, one of the ports visitors use to make their way to the Channel Islands, really embraced the dish. While you wait for your ferry, stop in at any number of local restaurants to sample some fish tacos, either deep-fried Baja style or grilled, like the one here.

YIELD: 4 SERVINGS
HANDS-ON TIME: 30 MINUTES
TOTAL TIME: 1 HOUR, INCLUDING MARINATING

JICAMA SLAW

2 limes, zested and juiced

1 tablespoon olive oil

2 teaspoons honey

1 teaspoon kosher salt

1 small jicama (about 8 ounces), peeled and cut into matchsticks

1½ cups finely shredded red cabbage

3 green onions, trimmed and thinly sliced

¼ cup fresh cilantro leaves and tender stems, chopped

FISH

2 teaspoons chili powder

1 teaspoon ancho chile powder or ½ teaspoon cayenne pepper

1¼ teaspoons kosher salt

4 (4- to 5-ounce) mahi-mahi fillets

2 tablespoons olive oil, divided

TACOS

8 to 12 corn tortillas

Crema or sour cream

Hot sauce

Lime wedges

1. To make the slaw, whisk together lime zest and juice, oil, honey, and salt in a medium bowl. Add jicama, cabbage, green onions, and cilantro. Toss until well combined. Marinate for at least 30 minutes or up to 2 hours.

2. To make the fish, preheat a grill or grill pan to medium-high heat. In a small bowl, combine chili powder, ancho chile powder, and salt. Pat fish dry with paper towels. Brush 1 tablespoon oil over fish, and coat with spice mixture, rubbing it into fish.

3. Brush grill or grill pan lightly with remaining 1 tablespoon oil. Grill fish, covered with grill lid, until opaque and fully cooked, 3 to 4 minutes per side. If desired, grill tortillas until warm and very lightly charred, about 10 seconds per side.

4. Flake fish into bite-size pieces. Serve fish in tortillas with slaw, crema, hot sauce, and lime wedges.

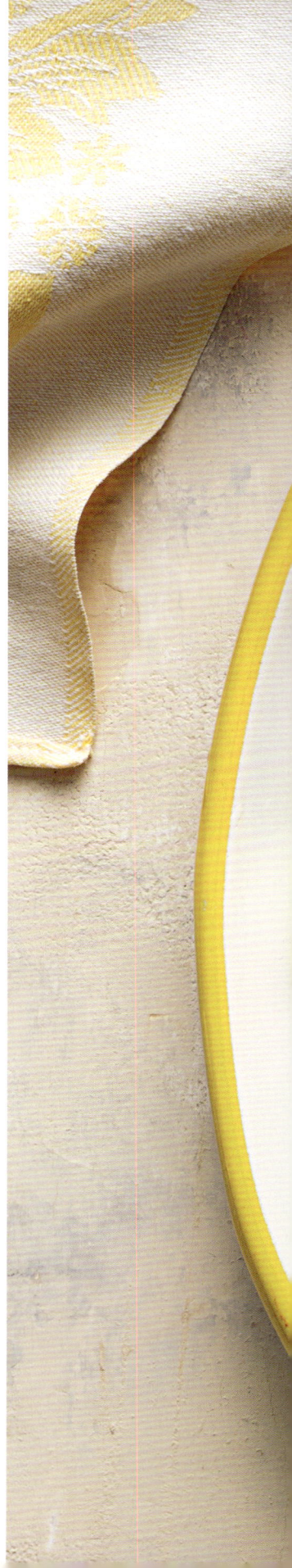

Anacapa and
Santa Cruz Islands

Shortcut Chilaquiles

You can do a lot of things on the five islands that make up Channel Islands National Park—surf, snorkel, camp, whale watch, kayak—but sitting down at a restaurant isn't one of them. Luckily, there are tons of great local spots near the ports in Ventura and Oxnard, California, where you grab a boat to the islands. A park visitors' favorite is Mrs. Olson's in Oxnard, where you'll find the tangy tomatillo breakfast chilaquiles—tortilla chips simmered in salsa, sometimes served with eggs—that inspired this recipe.

YIELD: 4 SERVINGS
HANDS-ON TIME: 10 MINUTES
TOTAL TIME: 35 MINUTES

Vegetable oil, for frying

12 corn tortillas, cut into 8 wedges each

¾ teaspoon salt, plus more for seasoning

2 (15.5-ounce) jars tomatillo salsa (about 3 cups)

1 cup chicken broth

½ teaspoon pepper, plus more for seasoning

1 cup (4 ounces) shredded pepper jack cheese

8 large eggs

2 tablespoons butter

For serving: thinly sliced radishes, crema or sour cream, sliced or chopped avocado, chopped fresh cilantro

1. Fill a large pot or deep skillet with enough oil to reach a depth of 2 inches. Heat oil over medium-high heat until it reaches 350°F. Set a wire rack inside a large baking sheet.

2. Working in batches, fry tortilla wedges in hot oil until light brown and crispy, about 1 minute per batch. Using a slotted spoon, transfer chips to prepared wire rack. Sprinkle with desired amount of salt while hot. Repeat with remaining tortillas.

3. In a large skillet, bring salsa and broth to a simmer over medium heat, and cook until hot. Add tortilla chips, stirring to coat, and simmer until softened to your liking, about 5 minutes for crisp-tender chips. Season with salt and pepper to taste. Top with cheese; turn off heat, cover, and keep warm.

4. In a medium bowl, beat eggs, ¾ teaspoon salt, and ½ teaspoon pepper until eggs are well blended. In a skillet, melt butter. Add eggs, and scramble, stirring frequently, until cooked to your liking.

5. Divide salsa mixture among 4 shallow bowls or plates. Add eggs and desired toppings. Serve immediately.

Smoky Collard Greens (page 69) and
South Carolina Pulled Pork With Mustard
Barbecue Sauce (page 68)

South Carolina Pulled Pork With Mustard Barbecue Sauce

The area around Congaree National Park is packed with barbecue joints that offer filling, casual meals after traversing the floodplain or paddling the 50-mile Congaree River Blue Trail. What sets South Carolina barbecue apart from other regional varieties is the sauce—simple yellow mustard is the main flavor driver. While proper southern pulled pork is often cooked in a pit, home cooks can create their own version with a from-scratch rub and a slow cooker. Serve it piled high on a bun and topped with bread-and-butter pickles, or on a platter with a side of Smoky Collard Greens (at right).

YIELD: 8 TO 12 SERVINGS
HANDS-ON TIME: 30 MINUTES
TOTAL TIME: 8 HOURS 30 MINUTES

PULLED PORK

2 teaspoons kosher salt, plus more for seasoning

1½ teaspoons ground mustard

1½ teaspoons brown sugar

1 teaspoon onion powder

1 teaspoon garlic powder

1 teaspoon smoked paprika

½ teaspoon pepper

5 pounds boneless pork butt

1 tablespoon vegetable oil

1 cup water

1 large yellow onion, quartered

MUSTARD BARBECUE SAUCE

1 cup yellow mustard

¼ cup white vinegar

3 tablespoons brown sugar

3 tablespoons ketchup

2 tablespoons light molasses, or 2 tablespoons brown sugar

1 tablespoon Worcestershire sauce

1 teaspoon garlic powder

¾ teaspoon pepper

½ teaspoon kosher salt

½ teaspoon onion powder

SERVE WITH

8 hamburger buns (optional)

Sliced bread-and-butter pickles (optional)

1. To make the pork, in a small bowl, combine salt, ground mustard, brown sugar, onion powder, garlic powder, smoked paprika, and pepper. Use fingers to break up any clumps.

2. Pat pork dry with paper towels. Rub spice mixture all over pork until completely coated. Heat oil in a large skillet over medium-high heat. Add pork, and cook until browned on all sides, about 8 minutes. Transfer pork to a slow cooker. (This step can be done entirely in the slow cooker if you have one with a sauté function.)

3. Add 1 cup water to skillet (or slow cooker) and bring to a simmer, scraping up any browned bits. If using skillet, pour liquid into slow cooker. Add onion. Cover, and cook on low until very tender, 8 to 10 hours.

4. Meanwhile, make the mustard barbecue sauce. In a medium pot, stir together all sauce ingredients. Bring to a boil over medium-high heat. Partially cover, reduce heat to medium-low, and simmer, stirring frequently, for 10 minutes. Turn off heat and cool completely. (Refrigerate in an airtight container if not using the same day. Bring to room temperature at least 1 hour before serving.)

5. Once pork is tender, discard all but 1 cup liquid in slow cooker, spooning off as much fat as possible. Transfer pork to a cutting board (preferably with grooves), and cool slightly, then chop or shred. Discard onion, or chop some with pork, if desired.

6. In a large bowl, toss together pork, chopped onion (if using), reserved liquid, and ½ cup barbecue sauce until coated. Taste, and add more sauce and salt, if needed.

7. Serve pork on buns with pickles (if desired) and mustard barbecue sauce.

Smoky Collard Greens

The southern edge of Congaree National Park is where the South Carolina Lowcountry begins, and with it a cuisine with its own delicious identity. One staple Lowcountry side—served alongside everything from shrimp and grits to barbecue—is collard greens. The large, fanlike leaves are slowly simmered with bacon until tender. A healthy tablespoonful of vinegar at the end of cooking adds a welcome pop of acidity that balances the rich, smoky dish.

YIELD: 8 TO 10 SERVINGS
HANDS-ON TIME: 40 MINUTES
TOTAL TIME: 1 HOUR 40 MINUTES

3 pounds collard greens
(3 or 4 bunches)

1 pound smoked thick-cut bacon, diced

1 medium sweet onion, diced

3 large cloves garlic, chopped

Pinch of crushed red pepper
(optional)

1 quart chicken stock or broth

4 cups water

Salt

1 tablespoon apple cider vinegar, or more to taste

Black pepper

1. Strip and discard stems from collard greens. Roughly chop collard leaves, place in a large pot, and fill with cold water. Use your hands to swirl leaves in water to release grit. Transfer leaves to a strainer, then repeat, rinsing one or two more times, until grit is gone. Don't worry about drying the leaves. Rinse and dry pot.

2. Place bacon in pot over medium heat. Cook, stirring occasionally, until bacon releases most of its fat but is not yet crisp, 6 to 8 minutes. Stir in onion and garlic; cook, stirring occasionally, until softened, 3 to 5 minutes. Stir in crushed red pepper, if using.

3. Increase heat to medium-high, and pour chicken stock and 4 cups water into pot. Bring to a boil, scraping bottom of pot to release any browned bits. Stir collard leaves into stock mixture in batches, stirring until wilted. Add a large pinch of salt, and return to a boil.

4. Reduce heat to medium-low, and partially cover pot. Simmer, stirring occasionally, until collard greens are cooked to your liking, 1 hour for tender greens and 1½ hours for very tender greens. There will still be liquid remaining (this is known as pot liquor and can be used as a dip for other elements of the meal). Stir in vinegar, then season everything in the pot with more salt and vinegar and black pepper to taste. Serve using a slotted spoon.

Recipe Note

Store leftovers in two airtight containers, one for the greens and one for the pot liquor, for up to 5 days.

Hazelnut–Chocolate Chip Bread Pudding

It's no wonder the hazelnut—or the filbert, as it was originally known—is the official nut of Oregon; the Pacific Northwest state produces an estimated 99 percent of all hazelnuts grown in the United States. Most of the 93,000 acres dedicated to the nut are in Willamette County, north of Crater Lake National Park, and it's the rich, volcanic soils, like those surrounding the park, that create these prime growing conditions. This bread pudding—a classic pairing of hazelnut and chocolate—was inspired by a guest-favorite recipe at Crater Lake Lodge, which has been serving park visitors 1,000 feet above the lake since 1915.

YIELD: 10 TO 12 SERVINGS

HANDS-ON TIME: 30 MINUTES

TOTAL TIME: 2 HOURS 15 MINUTES, INCLUDING SOAKING AND COOLING

1 loaf brioche bread (about 1 pound)

5 large eggs

2 cups (480 milliliters) whole milk

1 cup (240 milliliters) heavy cream

¾ cup (150 grams) plus 2 tablespoons granulated sugar, divided

2 teaspoons vanilla extract

½ teaspoon kosher salt

¾ cup hazelnuts

Butter, for greasing

1½ cups chocolate chips

Powdered sugar (optional)

1. Preheat oven to 300°F. Tear bread into roughly 2-inch pieces, and arrange in an even layer on a baking sheet (it's okay if the pieces overlap a bit). Bake 15 minutes; toss, and continue baking until dry and very lightly golden, 10 to 15 minutes more.

2. In a large bowl, beat eggs until blended; whisk in milk, heavy cream, ¾ cup sugar, vanilla, and salt until well combined. Add bread, gently stirring to completely coat; let soak at room temperature for 30 minutes.

3. Heat a small skillet over medium heat. Add hazelnuts and toast, stirring occasionally, until lightly browned in spots, about 5 minutes. Transfer nuts to a clean dish towel. Close towel and use it to rub off as much of the skins as possible. Chop nuts.

4. Increase oven temperature to 350°F. Grease a 9-by-13-inch baking dish with butter. Sprinkle remaining 2 tablespoons sugar on bottom of dish, and turn to coat sides. Pour out any excess.

5. Stir chocolate chips and hazelnuts into bread mixture. Transfer mixture into baking dish. Bake until bread pudding is puffed and custard is set (the bread won't jiggle and a toothpick will come out clean), 40 to 45 minutes.

6. Cool 10 minutes before serving; the bread pudding will deflate slightly as it sits. Dust with powdered sugar, if desired.

Crater Lake

Marionberry Grilled Cheese

The marionberry, a blackberry hybrid that was created in the mid-1900s, is quintessential Oregon. Marionberries appear on the menu at Crater Lake Lodge in the restaurant's triple-berry cobbler, along with raspberries and blueberries. The sweet-tart fruit also makes great jam, a common item in local gift shops. Here, the jam is used to take a simple grilled cheese up a notch (or three).

YIELD: 4 SANDWICHES
HANDS-ON TIME: 25 MINUTES
TOTAL TIME: 25 MINUTES

1½ cups shredded sharp cheddar cheese

1⅓ cups shredded fontina cheese

½ cup marionberry or blackberry jam or preserves

8 teaspoons Dijon mustard (optional)

8 thick slices sourdough bread

6 tablespoons unsalted butter

1. Heat a large cast-iron or non-stick skillet over medium heat. Toss together both cheeses in a bowl.

2. Spread jam and Dijon (if using) evenly on one side of each bread slice. Divide cheese among 4 slices, and top with remaining slices, jam sides down.

3. Place 2 tablespoons butter in skillet, swirling to coat. Add 2 sandwiches, press gently, and cook until the undersides are golden brown, 2 to 3 minutes. Flip, add 1 tablespoon butter to skillet, and cook until the second sides are golden brown, about 2 minutes. Transfer sandwiches to a clean surface. Repeat with remaining butter and sandwiches. Cool sandwiches for 1 minute before slicing in half.

Journalist William Gladstone Steel (far right) leads a party along the rim of Crater Lake in 1903.

Twice-Cooked Carrots With Cracked Coriander (page 77) and Trapp Family Farm Roasted Chicken (page 76)

Trapp Family Farm Roasted Chicken

A handful of sustainable livestock operations exist among the eight farms located within Ohio's Cuyahoga Valley National Park. Ben Bebenroth, chef-farmer of Spice Acres, points to his park neighbor, the Trapp Family Farm, as one of the best chicken producers in the area. The farm's pasture-raised birds freely roam their section of the valley (lucky visitors might find their eggs for sale at the self-serve farm stand, along with tomatoes, garlic, and okra). This roasted chicken is on regular rotation in Bebenroth's house, often served alongside his Twice-Cooked Carrots With Cracked Coriander (at right).

YIELD: 4 SERVINGS
HANDS-ON TIME: 30 MINUTES
TOTAL TIME: 1 HOUR 50 MINUTES

1 (4½-pound) whole chicken, preferably pasture-raised

Kosher salt

Freshly cracked pepper

1 head garlic, halved crosswise

4 sprigs fresh thyme

4 sprigs fresh oregano

1 sprig fresh sage

1 lemon, halved

1 teaspoon honey

1 to 2 tablespoons chopped fresh herbs (from any of the herbs above)

1. Preheat oven to 450°F.

2. Pat chicken dry with paper towels, and generously season inside of cavity with salt and pepper, turning to ensure a good coating. Place garlic halves, thyme, oregano, and sage inside cavity; plug with one lemon half, cut side facing in. Tuck wing tips underneath chicken and truss with kitchen twine. Generously season skin with salt and pepper. Transfer to a pan or baking dish, breast side up.

3. Roast chicken until fat begins to sizzle and top turns golden brown, about 30 minutes. Reduce heat to 325°F. Continue roasting until an instant-read thermometer inserted between breast and thigh reaches 160°F, about 30 minutes more.

4. Remove pan from oven, and tent with aluminum foil. Let rest 20 minutes, then transfer chicken to a cutting board (preferably grooved so juices can be saved as you carve it). Pour any juices from pan into a large measuring cup.

5. Remove and discard the twine as well as everything inside cavity. Carve chicken, separating breasts, legs, thighs, and wings. Cut breasts into slices against the grain. (Reserve the carcass for making stock another day, if desired.)

6. Pour any juices collected on cutting board into measuring cup. Stir in chopped herbs, honey, and juice from the remaining lemon half. Serve chicken immediately with sauce.

Twice-Cooked Carrots With Cracked Coriander

Nestled inside Cuyahoga Valley National Park are eight farms—a revitalization project of the late 1990s that aimed to return to the land's agricultural heritage and modernize it with sustainable practices. One of those farms is Spice Acres, managed by Ben Bebenroth, a chef-farmer who hosts educational programming and farm-to-table dinners on the property. When Bebenroth is off the clock, he cooks simple dinners for his family with the bounty he collects from farms in northeastern Ohio, including these carrots, which he makes with his house-dried coriander seeds.

YIELD: 4 SERVINGS
HANDS-ON TIME: 5 MINUTES
TOTAL TIME: 50 MINUTES

8 to 10 carrots with tops (about 1 pound)

Kosher salt

1 tablespoon coriander seeds

1 tablespoon olive oil

Freshly cracked pepper

1 tablespoon honey

1 tablespoon minced fresh chives

1. Trim carrot greens, leaving about 1 inch of tops; save a few leaves for serving. Place carrots in a pot that can easily hold them with room to move. Cover with cold water, and generously season with salt, just like you would for pasta.

2. Bring to a boil, uncovered, over high heat; reduce to a simmer. Cook until carrots are easily pierced with a toothpick, 25 to 30 minutes.

3. Meanwhile, place coriander seeds in a small pan over medium heat. Toast, stirring often, until fragrant and beginning to crackle, 2 to 3 minutes. (Reduce heat if starting to smoke.) Transfer to a plate to cool, then crack seeds with a mortar and pestle or by carefully pressing with the dull side of a chef's knife.

4. Heat broiler to high with oven rack set in the top-third position. Drain carrots, pat dry, and transfer to a baking sheet. Drizzle with oil, and sprinkle with salt and pepper. Broil until golden brown and blistered, about 7 minutes.

5. Toss carrots on the baking sheet with honey, cracked coriander, and chives. Serve immediately.

Death Valley National Park

With its distinct lack of forests and waterfalls, Death Valley defied the conventions of the time to become a national monument in 1933. It became a national park in 1994.

Spinach Salad With Prickly Pear Vinaigrette

Six species of prickly pear cactuses grow in California and Nevada's Death Valley National Park, including ones with fun names such as beavertail, old man, and grizzly bear. The cactus paddles are edible (see Ensalada de Nopales, page 200), as are the vibrant pink-red fruits. At the Oasis at Death Valley, the chefs use prickly pear fruit in many ways: in barbecue sauce, margaritas, and the vinaigrette in this salad. If you want to keep the cactus theme going, pick up some prickly pear chocolate, jelly, tea, or gummy bears at the resort's general store.

YIELD: 4 SERVINGS
HANDS-ON TIME: 15 MINUTES
TOTAL TIME: 15 MINUTES

PRICKLY PEAR VINAIGRETTE

⅓ cup prickly pear puree or syrup

2 tablespoons red wine vinegar

2 tablespoons Dijon mustard

1 shallot, minced

1 jalapeño pepper, seeded and minced

1 clove garlic, minced

⅓ cup light olive oil

Salt

SALAD

6 cups baby spinach

½ cup sweetened dried cranberries

¼ cup thinly sliced red onion, rinsed

½ cup sliced almonds, toasted

¼ cup crumbled goat cheese

1. To make the vinaigrette, add all ingredients except oil and salt to a tall, narrow container, such as a large tumbler or plastic quart container. Using an immersion blender, blend ingredients. With blender running, slowly drizzle in oil, blending until dressing is smooth. Season with salt to taste.

2. To make the salad, toss together spinach, cranberries, and onion in a large bowl. Drizzle with desired amount of dressing. Divide among 4 plates, and top with almonds and goat cheese.

Death Valley Date-Nut Bread

Visitors flock to Death Valley National Park, in California and Nevada, for the dramatic salt flats, the colorful and sculpted badlands, and the expansive desert views from Zabriskie Point. When folks need a little break from the park's extremes (it's the hottest and driest national park in the United States), they can find respite at the Oasis at Death Valley resort, which includes the Inn at Death Valley and the Ranch at Death Valley. The inn was originally built in 1927, and dates were the big crop for the ranch. You can get a taste of that history via the date bread served in the inn's dining room or sold at the ranch's general store. The caramelly bread, which has been a staple at the Oasis since the 1930s, is studded with walnuts and makes for a great hiking snack.

YIELD: 2 LOAVES

HANDS-ON TIME: 20 MINUTES

TOTAL TIME: 2 HOURS 20 MINUTES, INCLUDING SOAKING

---

2 cups pitted dates, chopped

1½ cups very hot water

4 cups (480 grams) all-purpose flour

1 cup walnuts, chopped

2 teaspoons baking soda

1 teaspoon kosher salt

½ cup (1 stick) butter, at room temperature

1 cup (200 grams) granulated sugar

1 cup (220 grams) packed brown sugar

1. In a large bowl, cover dates with hot water. Let stand 1 hour.

2. Preheat oven to 350°F. Line 2 loaf pans with parchment paper. In a medium bowl, mix flour, walnuts, baking soda, and salt until well combined. In another large bowl, beat butter, granulated sugar, and brown sugar with an electric mixer at medium speed until light and fluffy, about 3 minutes. Add dates and soaking liquid to butter mixture, and beat until blended. Add dry ingredients, and beat until just blended (do not overmix).

3. Divide batter between prepared loaf pans. Bake until a toothpick inserted into centers comes out clean, about 1 hour.

A horseback tour in the heart of Death Valley

Spruce Tip Shortbread Cookies

For nearly 20 years, Laura Cole owned and worked as the executive chef of 229 Parks, named for its location at mile 229.7 on the George Parks Highway near Denali National Park and Preserve. Cole's food drew locals and visitors alike with its focus on local ingredients. "For me, what is most important in cooking is the story you get to tell by the ingredients you use," says Cole. "Alaska is a state with great bounty for part of the year, and ice- and snow-covered for the rest of the year. It's very important to me to utilize all that we have here." She uses foraged spruce tips (edible young spruce tree needles, which home cooks can buy online) to make this fragrant sugar, a sweet and piney coating on these simple slice-and-bake shortbread cookies.

A view of Mount McKinley (Denali)

YIELD: 2 DOZEN COOKIES
HANDS-ON TIME: 20 MINUTES
TOTAL TIME: ABOUT 2 DAYS, INCLUDING DRYING

SPRUCE TIP SUGAR

½ cup finely chopped spruce tips or rosemary leaves

½ cup (100 grams) granulated sugar

COOKIES

10 tablespoons (1¼ sticks) unsalted butter, at room temperature

½ cup spruce tip sugar (at left), divided

¼ cup (30 grams) powdered sugar

½ teaspoon vanilla extract

1½ cups (180 grams) all-purpose flour

¼ teaspoon kosher salt

Recipe Note

To make these as Rose Water–Jam Cookie Sandwiches, in a small bowl, mix together ½ cup rhubarb jam and ½ teaspoon rose water. (Add a splash of water to loosen, if necessary.) Spread 1 teaspoon jam mixture on the bottom of a cookie, and top with a second cookie to form a sandwich.

1. To make the spruce tip sugar, mix spruce tips and sugar in a medium bowl until well combined. Spread in an even layer on a parchment paper–lined baking sheet, and let stand at room temperature, uncovered, until spruce tips are dry, 1 to 2 days. (The sugar can be made ahead and stored in an airtight container at room temperature for 3 months.)

2. To make the cookies, in a medium bowl, beat butter with an electric mixer at medium speed until fluffy, about 1 minute. Add ¼ cup spruce tip sugar and powdered sugar. Beat until well combined, 1 to 2 minutes, scraping down sides of bowl as needed. Beat in vanilla. Reduce speed to medium-low, and slowly add flour and salt, mixing until just blended.

3. Transfer dough to a large piece of plastic wrap, and shape it into a log about 7 inches long. Tightly wrap log, and chill at least 1 hour or overnight.

4. Preheat oven to 350°F. Line 2 baking sheets with parchment paper. Scatter remaining ¼ cup spruce tip sugar on a plate. Unwrap dough, and roll log in sugar, pressing to completely coat sides but not ends. Cut dough into ¼-inch-thick slices, and place about 1 inch apart on prepared baking sheets.

5. Bake, one sheet at a time, until lightly golden brown, 10 to 12 minutes. (Alternatively, bake on separate racks, rotating positions halfway through baking.) Let cool 3 minutes on baking sheets, then transfer to a wire rack to cool completely. Store in an airtight container for up to a week at room temperature, or freeze for up to 6 months.

Pork Tenderloin With Lingonberry Gastrique

Chef Laura Cole, for whom Alaska has been home for more than 20 years, calls Denali National Park and Preserve "the store outside my door." Her cooking features ingredients that are farmed, fished, ranched, hunted, or foraged locally. When you think of Alaska, you might not think of pork, but Cole uses meat that's ranched in-state. In this dish, she pairs pork tenderloin with a sweet and tangy sauce made with foraged berries. To make things easier for home cooks, jam stands in for the fresh Alaska fruit.

YIELD: 4 TO 6 SERVINGS
HANDS-ON TIME: 30 MINUTES
TOTAL TIME: 4 HOURS 10 MINUTES, INCLUDING COOLING AND MARINATING

4 cups plus 3 tablespoons water, divided

¼ cup plus 2 teaspoons birch syrup or maple syrup, divided

¼ cup Alaska or regular sea salt, plus more for seasoning

1 large sprig rosemary

1 tablespoon juniper berries, slightly crushed

2 to 2½ pounds pork tenderloin (2 tenderloins), silver skins removed

1 tablespoon Dijon mustard

2 tablespoons olive oil

1¼ cups lingonberry jam (one 12- to 14-ounce jar)

¼ cup apple cider vinegar

Pepper

1. In a large saucepan, combine 4 cups water, ¼ cup birch syrup, salt, rosemary, and juniper berries. Cook over medium heat, stirring constantly, until salt dissolves, 3 to 4 minutes. Turn off heat, and cool brine completely.

2. Place pork in a large zip-top plastic bag. Once brine has cooled, pour into bag over pork. Seal bag, and place in a large bowl. Chill at least 3 hours or overnight.

3. Preheat oven to 400°F. In a small bowl, mix Dijon and remaining 2 teaspoons birch syrup until smooth. Remove pork from brine, and pat dry with paper towels; discard brine. Brush pork all over with Dijon-syrup mixture.

4. In a large cast-iron or oven-safe skillet, heat oil over medium heat. Add pork, and brown, turning occasionally until browned all over, about 8 minutes total. Transfer skillet to oven, and roast until a meat thermometer inserted into thickest portion registers 140°F, 12 to 15 minutes. Transfer pork to a cutting board, tent with foil, and let stand while you make the gastrique. (The temperature will increase to 145°F.)

5. In a medium skillet, combine jam and 3 tablespoons water over medium heat. Bring to a simmer, and cook, stirring frequently, until jam bubbles and mixture is slightly reduced and thickened, about 5 minutes. Stir in vinegar, and return to a simmer. Cook, stirring frequently, until sauce coats the back of a spoon, 2 to 3 minutes. Turn off heat, and season gastrique with salt and pepper.

6. Thinly slice pork and serve with gastrique.

Four Marlins Salad With Key West Pink Shrimp

The only way to reach remote Dry Tortugas National Park is by boat or seaplane. And while you can camp on one of the park's seven islands, most visitors come for a day trip from the more inhabited areas of the Florida Keys. On Key West, a ferry departure point for a day at Dry Tortugas, diners can grab a taste of the tropics at Four Marlins restaurant in the Reach Key West hotel. The restaurant's namesake salad showcases some of the best food the archipelago offers, including hearts of palm, which grow wild on the islands, citrus, and the Key's own sweet, pink shrimp.

YIELD: 4 SERVINGS
HANDS-ON TIME: 25 MINUTES
TOTAL TIME: 40 MINUTES, NOT INCLUDING OVERNIGHT PICKLING

PICKLED ONION

½ cup rice wine or white wine vinegar

2 tablespoons granulated sugar

2 tablespoons kosher salt, plus more for seasoning

1 small red onion, thinly sliced

VINAIGRETTE

1 tablespoon rice wine vinegar

1 orange, zested and juiced

1 lime, zested

1 lemon, zested

1½ teaspoons Dijon mustard

1½ teaspoons honey

¼ teaspoon onion powder

¼ teaspoon garlic powder

2 tablespoons chopped fresh cilantro

½ cup vegetable oil

Salt and pepper

SALAD

1 (14-ounce) can whole hearts of palm, drained

2 tablespoons olive oil, divided

Salt and pepper

1 pound large Key West pink shrimp (or jumbo shrimp), peeled and deveined, tails on or off

1 (5-ounce) package mixed greens

1 pint heirloom cherry tomatoes, halved

1 orange, peeled and segmented

⅓ cup pepitas, toasted

3 ounces crumbled goat cheese

1. To make the pickled onion, in a small skillet, combine vinegar, sugar, and salt. Bring to a simmer over medium-high heat, stirring constantly, until sugar and salt are dissolved; turn off heat. Place onion in a heat-proof glass container. Pour hot liquid over onion and cover. Once cool, refrigerate overnight. (The pickled onion can be made ahead and stored in an airtight container in the refrigerator for up to 2 weeks.)

2. To make the vinaigrette, in a blender or food processor, combine all ingredients except oil, salt, and pepper. With blender running, slowly pour in oil until well blended. Season with salt and pepper.

3. To make the salad, preheat oven to 350°F. Pat hearts of palm dry, and gently toss on a baking sheet with 1 tablespoon oil and a large pinch of salt and pepper. Roast for 10 minutes. Cool for 5 minutes, then slice into ½-inch-thick pieces.

4. Pat shrimp dry with paper towels. Toss in a medium bowl with remaining 1 tablespoon oil and a large pinch of salt and pepper. Heat a large skillet over medium-high heat. Add shrimp, and cook until just firm and no longer opaque, 2 to 3 minutes per side. Transfer to a plate.

5. In a large bowl, toss together greens, tomatoes, orange segments, pepitas, desired amount of pickled onion, half the hearts of palm, half the vinaigrette, and a large pinch of salt and pepper. Divide among 4 shallow bowls or plates. Top with shrimp, goat cheese, remaining hearts of palm, and more pickled onion. Drizzle with more vinaigrette, if desired, and serve immediately.

Key Lime– Coconut Bars

If you're visiting Dry Tortugas National Park, chances are you'll come across Key limes on a menu during your Florida travels. This citrus is smaller than a typical lime but carries a bit more punch and a floral aroma. While Key limes haven't been commercially grown in the Keys since a hurricane blew through in the 1920s, local dishes still make a point to feature the iconic fruit. Fresh Key limes can be a little tricky to locate, but bottled juice is easy to come by. For a twist on classic Key lime pie, try these bars, which feature rich and creamy coconut— another staple on these islands—to offset the fruit's acidity.

YIELD: 16 BARS
HANDS-ON TIME: 15 MINUTES
TOTAL TIME: 5 HOURS, INCLUDING CHILLING

CRUST

1 cup (115 grams) graham cracker crumbs (about 7 or 8 whole crackers)

½ cup unsweetened coconut flakes

6 tablespoons coconut oil or unsalted butter, melted

¼ cup (55 grams) packed brown sugar

¼ teaspoon kosher salt

FILLING

6 large egg yolks

¼ cup (55 grams) packed brown sugar

1 (14-ounce) can sweetened condensed milk

Inside Ruins of Fort Jefferson Dry Tortugas, Key West, Florida

1 cup (8 ounces) unsweetened full-fat coconut milk (from a 13.5-ounce can; shake can well before measuring)

⅔ cup Key lime juice (about 5 ounces)

1 teaspoon regular lime zest

¼ teaspoon kosher salt

For serving: thinly sliced Key or regular limes, whipped cream

1. Preheat oven to 350°F. Line an 8-inch-square baking pan with parchment paper, leaving an overhang on all sides.

2. To make the crust, combine all ingredients until mixture looks like wet sand. Transfer to prepared pan, and firmly press into an even layer using the bottom of a measuring cup or glass. Bake until firm and color has slightly darkened, 10 to 12 minutes. Remove from oven to cool while preparing filling.

3. To make the filling, in a large bowl, beat egg yolks and sugar with an electric mixer on medium speed until lighter in color and thickened, 1 to 2 minutes. Beat in sweetened condensed milk, coconut milk, Key lime juice, lime zest, and salt until well blended.

4. Pour filling into slightly cooled crust. Bake until just set (the center will still jiggle), 30 to 35 minutes.

5. Transfer to a wire rack, cool completely, then cover with plastic wrap and chill for at least 4 hours or overnight. Slice into 16 squares, and serve with Key lime slices and whipped cream.

Everglades National Park — Lake Okeechobee in southeastern Florida is one of the largest freshwater lakes in the United States and has been a popular spot for fishing since the early 20th century.

EVERGLADES "GUIDE" SERVICE

CLEWISTON FLA.

Everglades National Park

Lake Okeechobee in southeastern Florida is one of the largest freshwater lakes in the United States and has been a popular spot for fishing since the early 20th century.

Mango-Passion-Banana Smoothie

Just outside Florida's Everglades National Park, you'll find Robert Is Here Fruit Stand and Farm, which has proudly occupied the same corner since 1959. The small shop specializes in rare and exotic tropical fruits, highlighting the region's cultural diversity and agricultural heritage. After a humid day searching the World Heritage site's wetlands for the endangered manatee, American crocodile, and Florida panther, hikers and bikers can stop by Robert Is Here for a milkshake or smoothie, like this one made with mango, passion fruit, and banana, staple crops that thrive in the area and are essential to the vibrant ecosystem.

YIELD: 1 SMOOTHIE

HANDS-ON TIME: 10 MINUTES

TOTAL TIME: 10 MINUTES

⅔ cup passion fruit juice

½ large mango, peeled, or 1 cup frozen mango

½ banana, peeled (fresh or frozen)

1 cup ice cubes, or more if needed

Honey (optional)

Mango slices and shredded coconut (optional)

1. In a blender, add passion fruit juice, mango, banana, and ice. Blend until smooth. Taste, then add honey for more sweetness, if desired, and more ice for a thicker smoothie. (If mango and banana are frozen, it will need less ice.)

2. Pour into a tall glass. Garnish with mango slices and shredded coconut, if desired.

A snowy egret flies over the park's grasslands.

Wild Blueberry Sourdough Waffles

North of the Arctic Circle in Alaska lies Gates of the Arctic, one of the most remote parks in the National Park System. Getting to the glaciated Arctic valleys, meandering rivers, and rocky peaks is a feat in and of itself, and transporting goods to this location is challenging. Learning how to live off the land—like the Iñupiat and Athabaskan people who have inhabited the area for thousands of years—is a critical skill that takes time to master. Come summer, locals forage wild berries. Using the berries in a pancake or waffle batter made with sourdough—a staple in Alaska—can be a real treat.

YIELD: 8 TO 12 WAFFLES

HANDS-ON TIME: 1 HOUR

TOTAL TIME: 1 HOUR, NOT INCLUDING CHILLING OVERNIGHT

1¼ cups (150 grams) all-purpose flour

1 cup (225 grams) unfed sourdough starter (also known as discard)

1 cup (240 milliliters) whole or 2% milk

2 tablespoons brown or granulated sugar

6 tablespoons (¾ stick) unsalted butter, plus more for serving

2 large eggs

1 teaspoon vanilla extract

1½ teaspoons baking soda

½ teaspoon kosher salt

2 cups wild blueberries (10 to 12 ounces), thawed if frozen

Maple syrup, for serving

1. In a large bowl, combine flour, sourdough starter, milk, and sugar. Mix until well combined, then cover tightly with plastic wrap, and refrigerate overnight.

2. The next day, heat waffle iron according to manufacturer's instructions.

3. Melt butter and cool for 5 minutes. In a medium bowl, beat eggs, then add cooled butter and vanilla. Pour egg mixture into flour mixture, stirring until just combined. Sprinkle in baking soda and salt, and stir until blended. (The batter might bubble and rise a bit.)

4. Grease waffle iron, then ladle in batter, and scatter a handful of blueberries on top. Cook according to manufacturer's instructions. Remove waffle from iron, and repeat with remaining batter and blueberries.

5. Serve waffles immediately with more butter, maple syrup, and any remaining blueberries.

Downtown St. Louis and the Gateway Arch

GATEWAY ARCH NATIONAL PARK

Gooey Butter Cake

The Gateway Arch became an instant St. Louis icon when it was completed in October 1965. Another St. Louis icon is gooey butter cake, which was first created by a local German American baker in the 1930s, some 17 years before Finnish American architect Eero Saarinen designed the arch. This recipe comes from St. Louis native Jessica Kimmell, who makes a version of her aunt Judy's recipe using a homemade yellow cake base, which bakes up more like a thick cookie.

YIELD: 12 SERVINGS
HANDS-ON TIME: 1 HOUR
TOTAL TIME: 1 HOUR 40 MINUTES, INCLUDING CHILLING

GOLDEN BUTTER CAKE BASE

1½ cups plus 3 tablespoons (205 grams) all-purpose flour

¾ teaspoon baking powder

⅓ teaspoon baking soda (heaping ¼ teaspoon)

⅓ teaspoon table salt (heaping ¼ teaspoon)

7½ tablespoons unsalted butter, very soft, plus more for greasing

1¼ cups (275 grams) packed light brown sugar

2 large eggs plus 1 egg yolk, lightly beaten

1½ teaspoons vanilla extract

1½ tablespoons milk

GOOEY TOPPING

1 (8-ounce) package cream cheese, at room temperature

2 large eggs, lightly beaten

2¾ cups (280 grams) powdered sugar, sifted, plus more for dusting

½ teaspoon vanilla extract

1. To make the cake base, in a medium bowl, mix together flour, baking powder, baking soda, and salt. In the bowl of a stand mixer fitted with the whisk attachment or in a large bowl using an electric mixer, beat butter and brown sugar at medium speed until well combined, about 2 minutes. Add eggs, vanilla, and milk. Mix until combined. Add dry ingredients, and mix until just combined.

2. Chill dough until it's the texture of slice-and-bake cookie dough, about 45 minutes. (If you're using a stand mixer, transfer cake base to another container so that you can use the mixer bowl to make the filling.)

3. Meanwhile, generously grease a 9-x-13-inch baking dish with butter and set aside. Preheat oven to 350°F.

4. To make the topping, beat cream cheese and eggs at medium speed until smooth. Add powdered sugar and vanilla. Beat until smooth.

5. When cake base is chilled, press it evenly into prepared pan. Make sure dough is not too thin in spots or the topping will leak through it.

6. Pour topping over cake base, and bake until topping is still a bit loose and shaky, 35 to 40 minutes. (Don't bake until topping is fully firm or the filling will be overcooked. The topping will firm up as it cools.) Let cake cool at least 1 hour, then lightly dust top with powdered sugar, and serve.

St. Louis–Style Toasted Ravioli

From the top of 630-foot Gateway Arch on a clear day, you can see as far as 30 miles, across views of downtown St. Louis to the west and Illinois to the east. The stainless steel– and carbon steel–plated monument is a symbol of the city and a favorite spot for visitors. Another St. Louis visitor favorite? A meal on the Hill, the city's historic Italian American neighborhood. One thing you'll notice on many menus here is toasted ravioli, a must-order appetizer, which, despite the name, is breaded and deep-fried.

YIELD: 4 APPETIZER SERVINGS
HANDS-ON TIME: 30 MINUTES
TOTAL TIME: 30 MINUTES

3 cups vegetable or peanut oil

¾ cup marinara sauce

1 large egg

1 tablespoon water

½ cup panko breadcrumbs

½ teaspoon kosher salt

½ teaspoon onion powder

½ teaspoon garlic powder

½ teaspoon dried oregano

1 (8- to 10-ounce) package refrigerated ravioli (any flavor)

Grated Parmesan cheese and chopped fresh parsley (optional)

1. In a large, heavy-bottomed pot, heat oil over medium-high heat until it reaches 350°F, about 10 minutes. Set a wire rack inside a large baking sheet, and place it next to the stove.

2. While oil heats, warm marinara in a small pan over medium heat, about 5 minutes. (Alternatively, microwave it until warm.) Cover sauce, and keep warm.

3. Beat egg in a medium bowl; beat in 1 tablespoon water. In another medium bowl, stir together panko, salt, onion powder, garlic powder, and oregano.

4. Working with one ravioli at a time, dip into egg mixture to coat, allowing excess to drip back into the bowl. Transfer to panko mixture, turning to coat evenly (the coating will be thin). Place coated pasta on a large plate. Repeat with remaining ravioli, egg mixture, and panko.

5. Gently add a few ravioli at a time to hot oil. (The number of ravioli will depend on the size of your pot, but you want enough ravioli to make a single layer with room between each one.)

6. Fry ravioli until golden on one side, about 30 seconds. Using a slotted spoon, gently turn each ravioli, and fry until golden on second side, about 30 seconds. Transfer to wire rack. Repeat with remaining ravioli, returning oil to 350°F between batches.

7. Transfer ravioli to a serving platter, and top with Parmesan and parsley, if desired. Serve with the warm marinara for dipping.

Huckleberry Arnold Palmer

Among Glacier's alpine lakes and towering peaks, you'll also find an abundance of plant species—grasses, ferns, lichens, and tasty things including six species of huckleberries. The blueberry-like fruit was widely used by the Blackfeet and other Indigenous tribes, who ate them both fresh and dried. Today, Glacier visitors can pick huckleberries during the summer and buy jars of sweet-tart huckleberry jam at many shops in the area. The spread is great on pancakes and is also a fun way to sweeten iced tea to make a Montana-inspired Arnold Palmer, a mix of half iced tea and half lemonade.

YIELD: 10 TO 12 SERVINGS
HANDS-ON TIME: 10 MINUTES
TOTAL TIME: 1 HOUR 20 MINUTES, INCLUDING COOLING

6 cups water

5 black tea bags

6 tablespoons huckleberry or blueberry jam

Ice

6 cups lemonade

Lemon slices

1. Bring 6 cups water to a boil in a saucepan. Add tea bags and let steep 8 minutes. Add jam, and stir until dissolved. Let tea cool, then chill at least 1 hour.

2. When ready to serve, fill glass with ice and then halfway with lemonade. Top with tea, slowly pouring it over the back of a spoon if you want to achieve a layered effect. Garnish with lemon slices.

A tour pauses with Grinnell Point in the distance.

Smoky S'mores Snack Mix

Whether you're camping, hiking, or driving the iconic Going-to-the-Sun-Road, there's one thing every visitor to Montana's Glacier National Park needs: good snacks. This combo is inspired by campfire s'mores, with graham cracker–flavored cereal as the base and smoked almonds playing the part of the crackling fire. Mini marshmallows are a must-have, and an assortment of pretzels, raisins, and chocolate chips rounds out the sweet, salty, and smoky treat. Think of this as less of a recipe and more of a starting point. Play around with the ingredients and ratios to create your ideal mix.

YIELD: ABOUT 3½ CUPS
HANDS-ON TIME: 5 MINUTES
TOTAL TIME: 5 MINUTES

2 cups graham cracker–flavored cereal, such as Golden Grahams

⅓ cup mini marshmallows

⅓ cup yogurt-covered pretzels

⅓ cup smoked almonds

⅓ cup chocolate-covered raisins

⅓ cup chocolate chips

1. In a large bowl, toss together all ingredients. Store in an airtight container up to 1 month.

Climbers ascend Stark Peak in 1926.

Teriyaki Black Cod With Seaweed Salad

More than 200 species of fish live in the waters of Alaska's Glacier Bay National Park and Preserve, which protects 1,200 miles of coastline and 950 square miles of ocean habitat. The bay's deepest point is 1,400 feet, which is ideal for species like the sablefish. The buttery, white-flesh fish is also known as black cod, despite having no relation to the cod family. Fatty sablefish is difficult to overcook, holds up well in a marinade, and is a perfect complement to seaweed, an edible marine plant that abounds in the bay.

YIELD: 4 SERVINGS
HANDS-ON TIME: 30 MINUTES
TOTAL TIME: 1 HOUR 30 MINUTES, INCLUDING COOLING AND MARINATING

BLACK COD

½ cup sake

½ cup mirin

½ cup soy sauce

¼ cup packed brown sugar

1 large clove garlic, grated

1 (1-inch) piece ginger, peeled and grated

4 (6- to 8-ounce) black cod (sablefish) fillets, skin on or off

Vegetable oil

SEAWEED SALAD

1 cup (1 ounce) dried wakame (about 2 cups once rehydrated; see note)

1 tablespoon rice vinegar

1 tablespoon toasted sesame oil

1 tablespoon ponzu or soy sauce

½ teaspoon brown sugar

SERVE WITH

Warm cooked jasmine rice

Sliced green onions

Toasted sesame seeds

1. To make the teriyaki sauce, in a medium skillet, stir together all ingredients except black cod and oil. Bring to a simmer over medium heat, stirring until sugar is dissolved. Continue simmering until the sauce is foamy and slightly syrupy, about 10 minutes. (This yields about 1 cup teriyaki sauce; it will continue to thicken to the consistency of maple syrup as it cools.) Transfer to a liquid measuring cup and cool to room temperature.

2. Once the sauce has cooled, transfer black cod to a large zip-top plastic bag. Add half the sauce, seal bag, and gently massage fish to coat. Marinate at room temperature for at least 30 minutes or up to 1 hour. Reserve remaining half of teriyaki sauce for serving.

3. Meanwhile, to make the seaweed salad, prepare wakame according to package directions. In a medium bowl, whisk together vinegar, sesame oil, ponzu, and brown sugar. When seaweed is ready, add it to vinegar mixture, and toss until well coated. Refrigerate until ready to serve.

4. Arrange oven rack in the top third of oven, and turn on broiler. Cover a baking sheet with aluminum foil, and coat lightly with vegetable oil. Remove fish from marinade; discard marinade. Place marinated fish evenly spaced apart on baking sheet. Broil until fish is cooked through and flaky, 7 to 9 minutes.

5. Arrange fish over rice, drizzle with reserved teriyaki sauce, and serve with seaweed salad. Sprinkle with green onions and sesame seeds.

Recipe Note

Wakame is an edible kelp native to the Pacific Ocean. Look for the dried version, used for *goma wakame* (Japanese seaweed salad), at Asian grocery stores or online.

Grand Canyon National Park

Established in 1919, Grand Canyon National Park has been welcoming adventure seekers to more than a million acres for generations.

Elk Bolognese

Located on the South Rim of the Grand Canyon, Arizona's historic El Tovar Hotel is a national parks icon. The property, which first opened in 1905, is made from limestone and Oregon pine and boasts a long celebrity guest list, including Theodore Roosevelt, Albert Einstein, and Oprah. El Tovar's dining room is also legendary: Murals represent the Hopi, Apache, Mojave, and Navajo peoples, and the menu reflects local influences, too, including the elk Bolognese, inspired by the herd that calls the park home.

YIELD: 4 SERVINGS
HANDS-ON TIME: 25 MINUTES
TOTAL TIME: 40 MINUTES

1½ tablespoons butter

⅓ cup finely chopped yellow onion

1 small carrot, finely chopped

1 small stalk celery, finely chopped

1 large clove garlic, finely chopped

12 ounces ground elk, venison, beef, or lamb

¼ cup dry red wine, such as merlot

2 tablespoons heavy cream

1 teaspoon Worcestershire sauce

2 cups marinara sauce

¼ teaspoon salt

Pinch of pepper

1 pound bucatini or spaghetti

For serving: small fresh mozzarella balls (perlini), freshly grated Parmesan cheese, thinly sliced fresh basil

1. In a large skillet, melt butter over medium-high heat. Add onion, carrot, and celery. Cook, stirring frequently, until vegetables soften, 3 to 4 minutes. Add garlic, and cook until fragrant, about 1 minute. Add elk, and cook until meat is brown, 4 to 5 minutes. Add wine, and stir, scraping up any browned bits on the bottom of skillet. Cook until wine reduces slightly, about 30 seconds. Reduce heat to medium-low, and stir in cream and Worcestershire. Simmer until flavors meld, about 15 minutes. Stir in marinara sauce, salt, and pepper. Let sauce simmer while you make the pasta.

2. Bring a large pot of salted water to a boil. Add pasta and cook according to package directions. Drain and return to pot. Add sauce, and toss until coated. Divide among 4 plates, and top with mozzarella, Parmesan, and basil.

El Tovar Blue Corn Pancakes With Pine Nut–Honey Butter

The pancake trio (buttermilk, Native American blue corn, and buckwheat pancakes) on the menu at El Tovar Hotel's dining room is delicious—and rich in history and tradition. The blue corn pancake, in particular, is deeply connected to the land in and around the Grand Canyon in Arizona. Corn, and blue corn in particular, is a sacred food for the Indigenous peoples of Arizona, including the Hopi, as a symbol of friendship, fertility, and family. Pairing the pancakes with the pine nut–honey butter is another nod to the place: Piñon trees grow in the Grand Canyon, where visitors can harvest as many as 25 pounds of nuts per day.

YIELD: 6 TO 8 PANCAKES
HANDS-ON TIME: 35 MINUTES
TOTAL TIME: 40 MINUTES

PINE NUT–HONEY BUTTER

½ cup (1 stick) butter, at room temperature

2 tablespoons honey

3 tablespoons toasted, cooled pine nuts, roughly chopped

Grand Canyon, early 1930s

BLUE CORN PANCAKES

¾ cup (100 grams) blue cornmeal

1 tablespoon sugar

1 teaspoon kosher salt

1 cup boiling water

½ cup (120 milliliters) milk

1 large egg

2 tablespoons butter, melted, plus more for cooking

2 teaspoons vanilla extract

¾ cup (90 grams) all-purpose flour

2 teaspoons baking powder

Maple syrup, for serving

1. To make the pine nut–honey butter, mix butter and honey using an electric mixer until fluffy, about 2 minutes. Stir in pine nuts until well blended.

2. To make the pancakes, mix together cornmeal, sugar, and salt

in a medium bowl. Stir in boiling water; cover and let stand until cornmeal softens, about 5 minutes.

3. Mix together milk, egg, butter, and vanilla in a small bowl until well blended. Whisk together flour and baking powder in another bowl until well blended.

4. When cornmeal is done soaking, add egg mixture, and whisk until blended. Add flour mixture, and stir just until combined.

5. Heat a medium skillet over medium heat. Add 1 to 2 teaspoons butter, and let it melt. Spoon about ⅓ cup batter onto skillet for each pancake, and cook until pancake looks dry on surface and bubbles burst and hold their shape, about 3 minutes. Flip and cook until browned, about 2 to 3 minutes longer. Repeat with remaining batter.

6. Serve with pine nut–honey butter and maple syrup.

Recipe Note

To serve the pancakes all at once, transfer cooked pancakes to a baking sheet in a 200°F oven to keep each batch warm while you continue to cook.

Signal Mountain Wild Game Chili

One of the main draws to Wyoming's Grand Teton National Park is wildlife-watching, and there sure is lots of it—from searching the sky for eagles to scanning the mountains for grizzly bears. In the heart of the park, adventurers looking to stay close to the wildlife can hang their hats at Signal Mountain Lodge and grab a bite at the Trapper Grill. The restaurant, which sits on the shore of Jackson Lake, serves up belly-warming bowls of wild game chili, a nod to some of the large mammals, including bison and elk, that roam the nearby land.

YIELD: 8 SERVINGS
HANDS-ON TIME: 15 MINUTES
TOTAL TIME: 1 HOUR

¼ cup vegetable oil

1 pound ground beef

1 pound ground bison

1 pound ground elk or venison

3 tablespoons onion powder

3 tablespoons garlic powder

3 tablespoons ancho chile powder

2 teaspoons ground cumin

1½ teaspoon kosher salt, divided, plus more for seasoning

1 (6-ounce) can tomato paste

2 (28-ounce) cans diced tomatoes

2 (15-ounce) cans black beans, drained

4 (4-ounce) cans diced mild green chiles

2 or 3 canned chipotle chile peppers in adobo sauce, chopped

2 teaspoons dried oregano

3 limes

For serving: shredded cheddar-jack cheese, sour cream, sliced green onions

1. In a large Dutch oven or heavy-bottomed pot, heat oil over medium-high heat. Add beef, bison, elk, onion powder, garlic powder, ancho chile powder, cumin, and ½ teaspoon salt. Break up meat with a wooden spoon, and cook, stirring occasionally, until meat is browned, 6 to 8 minutes.

2. Stir in tomato paste; cook until it starts to darken, about 2 minutes. Add diced tomatoes, beans, green chiles, chipotles, oregano, and 1 teaspoon salt. Bring to a boil, scraping bottom of pot to release any browned bits. Reduce heat to a low simmer, and cook for 30 minutes, stirring occasionally, to allow flavors to come together.

3. Add juice from 2 limes. Taste chili, and adjust seasoning with more salt and lime juice, if needed. Serve with desired toppings and remaining lime, cut into wedges.

Green Chile Breakfast Burritos

There's a lot to love aboveground at Nevada's Great Basin National Park: views of 13,065-foot Wheeler Peak; fishing and pine nut gathering; dark nights for stargazing; and hiking trails among gnarled, 1,000-year-old bristlecone pines. To put a cherry on top of (or below) it all, just underneath the surface lie Lehman Caves. Ranger-guided tours take visitors past stalactites, stalagmites, cave shields, and more along two miles of passageways. Before or after your tour, grab a bite at the Great Basin Cafe, the park's only restaurant. The cozy spot, which is open for breakfast and lunch, makes a great breakfast burrito filled with eggs, cheese, hash browns, and just-spicy-enough Hatch chiles.

YIELD: 2 BURRITOS
HANDS-ON TIME: 25 MINUTES
TOTAL TIME: 25 MINUTES

10 tablespoons olive oil, divided

6 cups frozen diced or shredded hash browns

1½ teaspoons kosher salt, divided

6 large eggs

1 cup grated sharp cheddar cheese

½ cup jarred or canned roasted Hatch green chiles (the café uses 505 Southwestern brand chiles)

2 burrito-size flour tortillas

2 tablespoons sour cream

1. In a large skillet, heat 2 tablespoons oil over medium heat. Add half of hash browns, spreading and pressing into an even layer. Cook until golden, about 5 minutes. Drizzle with 2 tablespoons oil, sprinkle with about ⅛ teaspoon salt (you can eyeball it), and flip. (It's okay if the hash browns break apart; just flip them in sections.) Sprinkle with another ⅛ teaspoon salt, then cook until golden and crispy, about 5 minutes. Transfer to a plate, and repeat the process with the remaining hash browns and ¼ teaspoon more salt.

2. Crack eggs into a medium bowl, season with 1 teaspoon salt, and whisk to blend. In same skillet, heat remaining 2 tablespoons oil over medium heat. Add eggs, and stir a few times. Top evenly with cheese and chiles, then continue cooking, stirring frequently, until eggs are cooked to your liking.

3. When eggs are almost done cooking, place tortillas in a microwave, and heat for 30 seconds on high (this will make it easier to roll up the burritos).

4. Divide sour cream between tortillas, spreading evenly. Top with hash browns and eggs. Roll up, burrito style.

5. Heat skillet over medium heat. Add burritos, and cook until lightly toasted, about 1 minute per side.

Wheeler Peak Overlook

Sandboarder Wraps

Of the two national parks to offer sandboarding and sledding, Great Sand Dunes in Colorado features the tallest dune (Star Dune, at 750 feet). Adventure seekers head to nearby rental shops between April and October to pick up equipment. (Snowboards and traditional sleds won't cut it.) Family-owned-and-operated Oasis, located just outside the park, has been catering to visitors since the mid-1980s, before Great Sand Dunes was declared an official national park and preserve in 2004. Besides rentals, the shop also has a restaurant offering wraps, like this one, to hungry boarders after riding the dunes.

YIELD: 4 WRAPS
HANDS-ON TIME: 25 MINUTES
TOTAL TIME: 25 MINUTES

CILANTRO-RANCH DRESSING

⅓ cup fresh cilantro leaves and tender stems, chopped

⅓ cup salsa verde

⅓ cup mayonnaise

⅓ cup buttermilk

1 clove garlic, minced

1 tablespoon ranch-flavored dry seasoning mix (from 1-ounce packet)

WRAPS

2 tablespoons vegetable oil

1 large yellow onion, chopped (about 2 cups)

1 to 1¼ pounds shaved beef or very thinly sliced sirloin

1½ teaspoons kosher salt

½ teaspoon pepper

4 spinach tortilla wraps

2 cups baby spinach

8 slices Swiss cheese

1. To make the dressing, combine all ingredients in a medium bowl until well blended.

2. To make the wraps, heat 1 tablespoon oil in a large nonstick skillet over high heat. Stir in onion; cook, stirring occasionally, until onion begins to brown, 2 to 3 minutes. Add remaining 1 tablespoon oil, then add beef in a single layer. Season with salt and pepper. Cook, stirring occasionally, to desired doneness, 2 to 4 minutes.

3. Place 1 wrap on a flat, clean surface; place one-fourth of beef mixture on the bottom third of wrap. Top with ½ cup spinach and 2 slices Swiss cheese. Drizzle with cilantro-ranch dressing. Tightly roll up wrap, tucking in ends. Slice in half diagonally. Repeat with remaining ingredients. Serve immediately with remaining dressing for dipping.

Pausing among the dunes

GREAT SMOKY MOUNTAINS NATIONAL PARK

Buttermilk Biscuits & Sawmill Gravy

The Great Smoky Mountains might be covered in forest now, but it was a much different story less than 100 years ago. In that era, farmers, settlers, and loggers cleared as much as 80 percent of the area. The sea of green that visitors enjoy today began its journey in only 1934, when the Smokies were designated a national park that spans North Carolina and Tennessee. One culinary holdover from the logging days is sawmill gravy, which was an easy and hearty dish to make in logging camps and for folks working in the sawmills. The creamy sausage gravy is almost always served with biscuits.

YIELD: 9 SERVINGS
HANDS-ON TIME: 50 MINUTES
TOTAL TIME: 50 MINUTES

2½ cups (300 grams) plus 3 tablespoons all-purpose flour, divided

2 teaspoons baking powder

1½ teaspoons granulated sugar

1½ teaspoons kosher salt, plus more for seasoning

½ teaspoon baking soda

½ cup (1 stick) unsalted butter, frozen, plus 3 tablespoons, divided

1 cup (240 milliliters) chilled buttermilk, plus more if needed

Flaky salt (optional)

1 pound country sausage (without casings)

2½ cups (600 milliliters) whole or 2% milk, plus more if needed

Freshly cracked black pepper

1. Preheat oven to 425°F.

2. In a large bowl, whisk together 2½ cups flour, baking powder, sugar, 1½ teaspoons kosher salt, and baking soda. Using the large holes of a box grater, grate ½ cup frozen butter, and add to flour mixture. Toss together with your hands, breaking up any large clumps of butter.

3. Make a well in the center of flour mixture. Pour in buttermilk. Using a fork, gently incorporate flour mixture and buttermilk, mixing until mostly combined.

4. Transfer dough to a lightly floured surface, and use your hands to knead it a few times until it comes together. Pat dough into a 1-inch-thick rectangle. Fold dough into thirds, starting from one long end, then press into a 1-inch-thick rectangle again. Fold into thirds a second time, then press dough into a

6-inch square. Cut into 9 equal squares. If desired, trim edges for flat sides.

5. Arrange biscuits, evenly spaced apart, in a 12-inch cast-iron skillet or on a baking sheet (if using a skillet, the biscuits will be a little snug). Melt 2 tablespoons butter, and brush over tops and sides of biscuits. Sprinkle with flaky salt, if desired.

6. Bake until tops are golden brown, 15 to 18 minutes.

7. Meanwhile, to make the gravy, melt remaining 1 tablespoon butter in a large skillet over medium-high heat. Add sausage, breaking it into small pieces with a spatula or spoon. Cook, undisturbed, until browned on bottom, about 3 minutes. Reduce heat to medium. Stir, breaking into smaller pieces, until fully cooked, 2 to 3 minutes.

8. Sprinkle sausage with remaining 3 tablespoons flour; mix until coated. Cook, stirring constantly, for 1 minute. Pour in milk, and bring to a simmer. Cook, stirring occasionally, until thickened, 2 to 3 minutes. Remove from heat, and season with salt and pepper. (If your gravy thickens too much, stir in a splash of milk to loosen it.)

9. Serve gravy immediately over sliced, warm biscuits. Sprinkle with more pepper, if desired.

Recipe Note

Ramps, a wild plant that tastes both oniony and garlicky, are foraged throughout Appalachia in the spring. If you can't find them at farmers markets or specialty groceries, use 1 medium leek (white and light green parts only, very thinly sliced) and 2 thinly sliced garlic cloves instead.

Foil-Wrapped Lemon-Pepper Trout

There are more than 2,900 miles of streams winding through Great Smoky Mountains National Park in North Carolina and Tennessee, brimming with more than 65 species of fish. Among those is the brook trout, the only trout species native to the park. Park visitors can fish the streams year-round (with proper permitting) to try to snag something for dinner. If you get lucky and catch a trout, the mild fish is delicious simply prepared with lemon, salt and pepper, some butter, and wild ramps. Wrap a fish fillet in foil to make it easy to cook on the grill or over the campfire.

YIELD: 4 SERVINGS
HANDS-ON TIME: 20 MINUTES
TOTAL TIME: 35 MINUTES

3 lemons

4 (¾-pound) butterflied, skin-on, boneless trout fillets (about 3 pounds total)

Olive oil

Salt and freshly cracked pepper

1 small bunch ramps, trimmed and roughly chopped (see note)

¼ cup (½ stick) cold butter, very thinly sliced

1. Zest 1 lemon and cut into wedges. Slice remaining 2 lemons. Preheat grill to medium-high heat or oven to 400°F. Tear off 4 large pieces of aluminum foil.

2. Pat trout very dry with paper towels. Drizzle both sides with oil to generously coat. Sprinkle skin with lemon zest, rubbing to adhere. Generously season trout on both sides with salt and pepper.

3. Lay 1 fillet open, skin side down, on a piece of foil. Top with one-fourth of the ramps on one side, and season with salt and pepper. Top with a few lemon slices and some butter; close fish. Wrap with foil, crimping tightly to seal. Repeat with remaining fish, ramps, salt, pepper, lemon slices, and butter.

4. Place foil-wrapped fish packets directly on grill, and cook, covered with grill lid and flipping packets once, until fish flakes easily with a fork, 12 to 15 minutes. Alternatively, bake foil packets on a baking sheet for 15 minutes. Cool 2 minutes, then carefully open foil. Transfer trout to plates, and drizzle with any juices in packets. Serve with lemon wedges.

Cherry-Chipotle Brownies

For centuries, the Frijole Ranch area in what is now Guadalupe Mountains National Park was a place many called home. Petroglyphs, artifacts, and mescal pits let us know that Native Americans once lived in the area, and over the years ranches, homes, and even a schoolhouse were added. One family, the Smiths, lived on the property for nearly 40 years and raised 10 kids. They had a 15-acre orchard and garden, which included apples, plums, pears, and even a few cherry trees. The dried cherries in these brownies are an homage to that orchard, and the smoky chipotle powder is a nod to the cuisine of New Mexico (just north of the park) and Mexico (just west of the park).

YIELD: 9 TO 12 SERVINGS

HANDS-ON TIME: 20 MINUTES

TOTAL TIME: 1 HOUR, NOT INCLUDING COOLING

6 tablespoons unsalted butter, cut into cubes, plus more for greasing

Boiling water

⅔ cup dried cherries

½ cup (60 grams) all-purpose flour

⅓ cup (32 grams) unsweetened cocoa powder

¾ teaspoon chipotle chile powder

½ teaspoon kosher salt

½ teaspoon ground cinnamon

El Capitan at sunrise

4 ounces semisweet chocolate from a baking bar, chopped

¾ cup (150 grams) sugar

2 large eggs

1 teaspoon vanilla extract

⅔ cup semisweet chocolate chips or chunks

1. Preheat oven to 325°F. Grease an 8-inch-square pan with butter, and cover bottom with parchment paper, leaving an overhang on two sides.

2. In a heatproof bowl or glass measuring cup, pour boiling water over cherries until just covered. Let stand 10 minutes, then drain.

3. Meanwhile, in a small bowl, whisk together flour, cocoa powder, chipotle chile powder, salt, and cinnamon.

4. In a small pot, bring 1 inch of water to a simmer. In a heatproof bowl that fits snugly on top of the pot, add 6 tablespoons butter and the chopped chocolate. Stir until melted, 2 to 3 minutes. Remove from heat.

5. Place sugar in a large bowl, then slowly whisk in melted chocolate mixture until just combined. Add eggs, one at a time, whisking until just combined. Whisk in vanilla. Using a silicone spatula, stir in flour mixture until just combined. Stir in drained cherries and chocolate chips.

6. Transfer batter to prepared pan, smoothing the top. Bake until a toothpick comes out with just a few crumbs on it, 30 to 35 minutes. Cool completely in pan before removing the parchment sling, and slice into squares.

Pipikaula

Recipe adapted with permission from *Cook Real Hawai'i*
by Sheldon Simeon with Garrett Snyder

Ranching on Hawai'i dates back to the 1830s, when King Kameha-meha III invited a group of Mexican vaqueros (cowboys) from Califor-nia to train Hawaiian ranch hands to rope and work cattle. As the cattle industry boomed over the next century, the hard-riding paniolo (native Hawaiian cowboy) became an iconic figure in local culture. Paniolos loved chewing pipikaula, a sun-dried beef jerky meant to last through long rides. This version (baked in the oven rather than by the sun) pays homage to paniolo history—as well as the Hawaiian sun, which draws Haleakalā's visitors to the volcano's peak in the earliest hours of the day.

YIELD: ABOUT 1 POUND
HANDS-ON TIME: 10 MINUTES
TOTAL TIME: 5 HOURS 10 MINUTES

2 pounds flank steak

3 tablespoons kosher salt

2 tablespoons shoyu (soy sauce)

1 tablespoon kudeesh sauce (at right), or more to taste

2 teaspoons freshly cracked black pepper

1. Preheat oven to 200°F. Cover a baking sheet with aluminum foil, then place a wire rack on top.

2. Massage flank steak enthusias-tically with salt for several minutes. In a small bowl, combine shoyu, kudeesh sauce, and pepper; coat steak evenly with mixture.

3. Place steak on prepared wire rack. Bake until dried but tender, 6 to 7 hours. (The inside should appear medium to medium-well.) Tear steak into ½- to ¾-inch strips with the grain. Store in an airtight container in the refrigerator for up to 1 month.

Sunset at 10,023 feet

Kudeesh Sauce

Kudeesh sauce can be used as an all-purpose hot sauce with fried noodles or rice.

YIELD: ABOUT ¼ CUP
HANDS-ON TIME: 5 MINUTES
TOTAL TIME: 5 MINUTES

½ cup (about 1 ounce) assorted hot fresh chiles (such as Hawaiian, bird's-eye, and red Fresno), sliced or coarsely chopped

2 tablespoons apple cider vinegar

1 tablespoon granulated sugar

1½ teaspoons kosher salt

1. In a blender or mini food processor, combine all ingredients, and process until a smooth sauce forms, 3 to 4 minutes. (Be careful not to breathe in any fumes when you open the container.)

Pork & Sweet Onion Manapua

There's no food sold at Hawai'i's Haleakalā National Park, which means visitors have to pack their own provisions before exploring the wilderness trails, camping, or chasing the sunrise at the summit of the dormant volcano. At local bakeries, keep an eye out for *manapua*, stuffed steamed or baked buns, similar to Chinese *bao*, which make for the perfect packable meal. The pastries can be filled with various things, but this version from Maui-based chef Rosalinda Mariotti is stuffed with a delicious combo of SPAM® canned pork and Maui onions.

YIELD: 10 MANAPUA
HANDS-ON TIME: 1 HOUR
TOTAL TIME: 4 HOURS

DOUGH

2 large eggs

1 cup (240 milliliters) plus 1 tablespoon milk, divided

¼ cup (55 grams) packed brown sugar, divided

2 teaspoons instant yeast

4 cups (520 grams) bread flour

⅓ cup vegetable oil

1 teaspoon kosher salt

Furikake seasoning

FILLING

2 tablespoons vegetable oil

2 medium Maui or other sweet onions, diced

2 large cloves garlic, minced

½ cup pineapple juice or ½ cup water plus 1 tablespoon granulated sugar

½ cup char siu sauce, teriyaki sauce, or Japanese barbecue sauce

1 tablespoon mirin or dry sherry

1 tablespoon soy sauce

2 teaspoons cornstarch

1 teaspoon toasted sesame oil (optional)

1 (12-ounce) can SPAM canned pork, diced into ¼-inch cubes

Kosher salt

1. To make the dough, beat 1 egg. Separate remaining egg, reserving yolk (discard or save egg white for another use). In a small, microwave-safe bowl, heat ¼ cup milk and 1 tablespoon brown sugar for 30 seconds (it should register between 105°F and 115°F on an instant-read thermometer). Stir to dissolve sugar. Pour milk mixture into bowl of a stand mixer fitted with a dough hook; sprinkle yeast on top. Let stand until yeast begins to foam, about 5 minutes.

2. Add flour, ¾ cup milk, remaining 3 tablespoons brown sugar, oil, beaten egg, and salt. Beat on medium-low speed until dough comes together and starts to move up the hook, 3 to 5 minutes. Cover dough with a clean kitchen towel, and place in a warm area until doubled in size, about 2 hours.

starch, and sesame oil (if using) until smooth.

5. Stir SPAM canned pork into caramelized onions. Cook, stirring occasionally, until meat is heated through, 1 to 2 minutes. Pour sauce into skillet, and mix until coated. Bring to a simmer over medium heat, and cook until sauce is thickened and glossy, 2 to 3 minutes. Transfer to a bowl or small baking dish, and cool completely. Cover and chill. (The filling can be made up to 5 days in advance.)

6. Line a baking sheet with parchment paper. Punch down dough and turn out onto a lightly floured surface. Divide into 10 equal portions (80 to 85 grams each). Cover dough with a towel to keep it from drying out.

7. Roll out each portion of dough into a 6-inch circle, leaving centers a bit thicker than edges to help create an even bun after you fill them.

8. Spoon ¼ cup filling onto center of each disk. Bring edges of dough around filling to enclose it, and pinch edges tightly to seal. Place dough on prepared baking sheet, seam side down, and cover with towel. Repeat with remaining dough and filling. Let rise in a warm spot until puffy, 30 minutes to 1 hour.

9. Preheat oven to 350°F. In a small bowl, beat reserved egg yolk with remaining 1 tablespoon milk. Brush each bun with egg wash, then sprinkle with furikake.

10. Bake until buns are golden brown and cooked through, 20 to 22 minutes, rotating pan halfway through cooking. Serve warm.

3. Meanwhile, to make the filling, heat oil in a large skillet over medium heat. Add onions, and cook, stirring occasionally, until softened, about 5 minutes. Reduce heat to medium-low, and cook, stirring occasionally, until onions caramelize, 20 to 25 minutes. If the onions start to brown too quickly, lower the heat and add a splash of water to skillet.

4. In a small bowl, whisk together garlic, pineapple juice, char siu sauce, mirin, soy sauce, corn-

Hawai'i Volcanoes National Park

Visitors to the park can walk the hardened lava flows from the 1969–1974 eruption of Maunaulu, shown here spewing lava into 'Ālo'i crater. The eruption lasted 1,774 days and sent lava fountains 1,770 feet into the air.

Chicken Katsu

Japanese immigrants came to Hawai'i in 1885, landing on Oahu to work on sugarcane and pineapple plantations. The population expanded to the other islands, including the Big Island. At its peak in the 1940s, an estimated 37 percent of the Big Island's population was Japanese; that number has dropped, but the cultural impact remains. On the islands, Japanese food abounds, and after a hike through rugged Hawai'i Volcanoes National Park, a plate of expertly fried chicken katsu over rice might be exactly what your body needs.

YIELD: 4 SERVINGS
HANDS-ON TIME: 40 MINUTES
TOTAL TIME: 40 MINUTES

¼ cup rice vinegar

1 tablespoon toasted sesame oil

2 teaspoons honey

4 cups shredded napa or green cabbage (½ medium head)

4 green onions, thinly sliced

1½ teaspoons kosher salt, plus more for seasoning

4 boneless, skinless chicken thighs (about 1½ pounds)

Pepper

½ cup all-purpose flour

2 large eggs

1¼ cups panko breadcrumbs

1 tablespoon shichimi togarashi (Japanese seven-spice blend), optional

Vegetable oil

Katsu sauce

Toasted sesame seeds (optional)

1. In a medium bowl, whisk together vinegar, sesame oil, and honey. Add cabbage, green onions, and 1½ teaspoons salt. Toss until cabbage is coated; let marinate at room temperature while preparing the rest of the meal.

2. Meanwhile, pat chicken dry with paper towels. Place thighs, one at a time, between two large pieces of plastic wrap on a cutting board. Using a meat mallet, pound thighs to ½-inch thickness. Season lightly on both sides with salt and pepper.

3. Mix together flour and a large pinch of salt and pepper in a shallow bowl. Place eggs in a second shallow bowl; beat. Place panko, shichimi togarashi (if using), and a large pinch of salt in a third shallow bowl.

4. Coat chicken thighs, one at a time, in flour mixture, gently shaking off excess. Dip in eggs, allowing excess to drip back into dish. Finally, coat with panko mixture, turning several times. Transfer to a clean plate.

5. In a large skillet, heat a thin layer of oil (about ¼ inch deep) over medium-high heat. Once oil is shimmering, add 2 coated thighs to skillet. Fry, turning once, until browned and cooked through, 3 to 4 minutes per side. Transfer to a cutting board, and repeat with remaining chicken.

6. Slice chicken into strips, and transfer to individual plates. Drizzle with katsu sauce. Serve with the cabbage, and sprinkle with sesame seeds, if desired.

Tuna Poke

Encompassing the summits of Kīlauea and Mauna Loa—two of the world's most active volcanoes and sacred spots for Native Hawaiians—Hawai'i Volcanoes National Park is a site (and a sight) to behold. While staying at the Volcano House on park property, visitors can grab a bite at the Rim restaurant, which overlooks the Kīlauea caldera. The menu is inspired by the local cuisine, including a take on one of the state's signature dishes, tuna poke. Here, the fish is prepared with more of a traditional approach. Serve it as is, or round out the meal with cooked rice, cucumber, and avocado.

YIELD: 4 SERVINGS
HANDS-ON TIME: 20 MINUTES
TOTAL TIME: 1 HOUR 20 MINUTES, INCLUDING CHILLING

1 pound sushi-grade tuna, cut into ¾-inch cubes

4 green onions, thinly sliced, divided

¼ cup very thinly sliced Maui or other sweet yellow onion

¼ cup macadamia nuts, very finely chopped, divided

4 teaspoons toasted sesame seeds, divided

1 tablespoon nori (seaweed) flakes

3 tablespoons shoyu or soy sauce

1 tablespoon toasted sesame oil

½ teaspoon coarse sea salt

½ teaspoon crushed red pepper (optional)

Furikake seasoning

For serving: warm cooked rice, diced cucumber, and avocado (if making it a main dish)

Lava flows meet the coast.

1. In a medium serving bowl, combine tuna, 2 tablespoons green onions, Maui onion, 2 tablespoons nuts, 2 teaspoons sesame seeds, nori flakes, shoyu, sesame oil, salt, and crushed red pepper (if using). Gently toss until tuna is coated.

2. Cover bowl and refrigerate for 1 hour. Garnish with remaining green onions, nuts, and sesame seeds. Sprinkle with furikake. Serve as an appetizer, or as a main dish with rice, cucumber, and avocado.

Smash Burgers

Hot Springs National Park offers a glimpse into the past with eight bathhouses of the kind that once made Arkansas a sought-after wellness resort destination. You can still experience the healing mineral waters in two of the original bathhouses—as well as spas in and around the park—or embrace nature at the campground on Gulpha Creek and along 26 miles of hiking trails. The remaining six bathhouses have been repurposed for various uses (a hotel, park offices, a visitors center), but only one is now a brewery and restaurant. Beer brewed with spring water is the big draw at Superior Bathhouse Brewery, and you'd be remiss if you didn't pair your pint with a smash burger.

YIELD: 4 DOUBLE CHEESEBURGERS
HANDS-ON TIME: 20 MINUTES
TOTAL TIME: 1 HOUR

KILLER ONIONS

3 tablespoons olive oil

3 medium yellow or white onions (1½ pounds), thinly sliced

Kosher salt

¼ cup Irish red lager (such as Killian's)

BURGER SAUCE

½ cup mayonnaise

3 tablespoons ketchup

½ teaspoon granulated garlic

½ teaspoon paprika

½ teaspoon pepper

1 tablespoon canned roasted jalapeño peppers, finely chopped (see note)

1 large clove garlic, finely chopped

3 tablespoons sweet pickle relish

SMASH BURGERS

2 pounds ground beef

Kosher salt and pepper

¼ cup olive oil

8 thin slices American cheese (see note)

4 brioche burger buns, toasted

For serving: lettuce, tomato slices, and pickle slices

1. To make the killer onions, heat oil in a large skillet over medium heat. Add onions, and cook, stirring constantly, until beginning to soften, about 5 minutes. Sprinkle with salt, stir well, and reduce heat to medium-low. Continue to cook, stirring occasionally, until onions are very soft and caramelized, about 45 minutes. (Reduce heat to low if onions begin to brown too quickly, and add a drizzle of oil if they're sticking.) Add beer, and stir, scraping up browned bits on bottom of skillet. Cook until beer is slightly reduced, about 30 seconds.

2. To make the sauce, add all ingredients except relish to a blender or mini food processor,

and blend or pulse until mixture is mostly smooth. (If you prefer a chunkier sauce, mix the ingredients in a bowl until well combined.) Stir in relish.

3. To make the burgers, divide beef into 8 equal portions, and roll into balls. Place on a baking sheet, and season generously with salt and pepper.

4. Heat 2 tablespoons oil on a griddle or large cast-iron or other nonstick skillet over medium-high heat. Coat a metal spatula with oil or cooking spray. Cook half of beef in hot oil, until browned on bottom, about 4 minutes. Press beef firmly with spatula to create thin patties (you might need to press them more than once).

5. Flip patties, press again with spatula, then top each with 1 slice of cheese. Cover pan with a lid or foil, and cook until cheese is melted, about 2 minutes. Repeat with remaining patties and 2 tablespoons oil.

6. Serve 2 burger patties stacked on each bun with burger sauce, lettuce, tomato slices, killer onions, and pickle slices. Serve with remaining sauce alongside.

Recipe Note

You can substitute 1 small fresh jalapeño pepper for the canned peppers; roast it over a gas flame or broil it before seeding and chopping it. If you prefer blue cheese, substitute 6 ounces for the American cheese slices.

Beer Cheese Dip

If you want a true taste of Arkansas's Hot Springs National Park, you need to stop by Superior Bathhouse Brewery. It's the only brewery located in a national park, *and* it serves the world's only beer brewed with thermal spring water. Choose from 18 thermal spring water craft beers on tap inside the 1916 building, originally the smallest of the eight bathhouses in the park. The brewery also offers lunch, dinner, and snacks, such as a soft pretzel with a side of beer cheese dip made with the brewery's Spring Training blonde ale.

YIELD: 8 SERVINGS
HANDS-ON TIME: 15 MINUTES
TOTAL TIME: 15 MINUTES

2 tablespoons unsalted butter

2 tablespoons all-purpose flour

⅔ cup beer (blonde ale or lager)

½ cup whole or 2% milk

¼ cup heavy cream

½ teaspoon all-purpose seasoning

5½ ounces deli-sliced white American cheese, cut into ½-inch pieces (about 1¼ cups)

Tortilla chips or soft pretzels

1. In a medium saucepan, melt butter over medium heat. Sprinkle in flour, and whisk until mixture turns light golden, about 2 minutes.

2. Reduce heat to low, and whisk in beer, milk, cream, and all-purpose seasoning. Cook, whisking frequently, until steaming, about 3 minutes.

3. Gradually sprinkle small handfuls of cheese over milk mixture, whisking constantly until cheese melts completely after each addition. Cook, whisking constantly, until dip is smooth and falls in thick ribbons from a spoon, about 5 minutes.

4. Transfer dip to a small bowl. Serve immediately with chips or pretzels.

Diana of the Dunes Latte

This coffee drink was created as a tribute to Alice Mabel Gray (nicknamed Diana of the Dunes), a mathematician and astronomer who left behind Chicago's city life in 1915 to embrace the wild beauty of what is now Indiana Dunes National Park. Her legacy is one of resilience, independence, and advocacy for the preservation of the dunes, a mission that ultimately contributed to the establishment of the park. Gray's story deeply resonates with Alison Scates, co-owner of Fluid Coffee Roasters in nearby Michigan City, Indiana, where the Diana of the Dunes Latte—made with a simple syrup infused with local lavender—is a permanent fixture on the menu. Scates says the drink serves as an empowering reminder of the strength and spirit of women who dare to chart their own paths.

YIELD: 1 LATTE

HANDS-ON TIME: 5 MINUTES

TOTAL TIME: 10 MINUTES, NOT INCLUDING SIMPLE SYRUP

2 shots espresso (see note)

1½ ounces lavender simple syrup (at right)

8 ounces dairy or nondairy milk of choice (see note)

Lavender sprig (optional)

1. In a large coffee mug, gently mix together espresso and lavender simple syrup.

2. Heat milk in a steamer until frothy, then pour over sweetened espresso. Add a sprig of lavender, if desired. Serve immediately.

Lavender Simple Syrup

YIELD: 1⅔ CUPS

HANDS-ON TIME: 5 MINUTES

TOTAL TIME: 20 MINUTES

2 tablespoons dried lavender buds

1 cup boiling water

1 cup sugar

¼ teaspoon lemon extract

1. Place dried lavender buds in a heatproof measuring cup. Top with boiling water. Cover and steep 15 minutes.

2. Place a small fine-mesh strainer over a second measuring cup or nonreactive bowl; pour to strain, and discard lavender. Stir in sugar until dissolved. Stir in lemon extract. Cool, then transfer to an airtight container. Store in refrigerator for up to 2 weeks.

Native wildflowers

Recipe Note

If you don't have access to
an espresso machine, this
recipe can also be made
with 6 ounces cold brew
or filter-brewed coffee,
1½ ounces lavender simple
syrup, and 6 ounces milk.
Fluid Coffee Roasters recom-
mends barista-style oat milk,
but any dairy or nondairy
milk will work here.

Smoked Whitefish Dip

In the far northern reaches of Lake Superior lies Isle Royale National Park, an isolated Michigan island that borders Canadian territory. Fishing enthusiasts flock to the rugged landscape to hook more than 40 documented species, including the cold-water-loving lake whitefish. For years, locals have smoked the whitefish as a way to preserve a high-protein food source through the island's harsh winters. The smoked fish has made its way into creamy dips throughout Michigan, like this one, inspired by the one at Rock Harbor Lodge and Lighthouse Restaurant in the park.

YIELD: 8 SERVINGS
HANDS-ON TIME: 15 MINUTES
TOTAL TIME: 1 HOUR 15 MINUTES, INCLUDING CHILLING

6 ounces cream cheese, softened

2 green onions, trimmed and minced

2 tablespoons chopped fresh dill, plus more for serving

2 tablespoons drained capers, coarsely chopped

2 tablespoons mayonnaise

1 lemon, zested and juiced

1 teaspoon Worcestershire sauce

½ teaspoon garlic powder

Pinch of cayenne pepper or hot sauce (optional)

Kosher salt

7 to 8 ounces smoked whitefish, flaked into large pieces, skin and bones discarded

Crackers or flatbread

1. In a medium bowl, combine cream cheese, green onions, dill, capers, mayonnaise, lemon zest and 1 tablespoon lemon juice, Worcestershire, garlic powder, and cayenne (if desired). Beat at medium speed using an electric mixer until well combined. Add salt to taste, and adjust lemon juice and cayenne, if necessary.

2. Add whitefish. Beat on low speed until just combined, about 15 seconds. (Do not overbeat.) Transfer to a 2-cup serving dish, and spread in an even layer. Cover dip with plastic wrap, and refrigerate for at least 1 hour before serving. (You can make the dip up to 2 days ahead.)

3. Sprinkle with fresh dill before serving. Serve with crackers or flatbread.

Calm waters before departure

Pappy & Harriet's Tri-Tip Sandwich

About a half hour from Joshua Tree National Park, you'll find Pioneer-town, California, a Western movie set and living town built in the 1940s for legends like Gene Autry and Roy Rogers. In the 1940s and '50s, what would become Pappy & Harriet's restaurant was the location for saloon and shootout scenes. When the Western craze was over and the crews left, the location became a burrito bar for outlaw bikers, and after the restaurant was founded in 1982, it morphed into a spot known for live music (Paul McCartney, Lucinda Williams, and Glass Animals have played there). It also became legendary for next-level California-style barbecue, including the fan-favorite tri-tip sandwich, which comes with cheese, grilled onions, and Pappy & Harriet's famous barbecue sauce.

YIELD: 6 SANDWICHES

HANDS-ON TIME: 30 MINUTES

TOTAL TIME: 1 HOUR, INCLUDING STANDING

1 tablespoon kosher salt, plus more for seasoning

1 tablespoon garlic powder

1 tablespoon pepper

3 pounds tri-tip or sirloin steak

1 large red onion, cut into ½-inch-thick rounds

2 tablespoons olive oil or other vegetable oil, plus more for drizzling

6 French rolls, sliced

2 cups (8 ounces) grated cheddar cheese

Barbecue sauce

Hidden Valley Campground in 1957

144

1. In a small bowl, mix together salt, garlic powder, and pepper. Rub all over tri-tip. Let meat marinate at room temperature for 30 minutes.

2. Meanwhile, preheat grill to medium-high heat (375°F to 400°F), creating one hot zone and one cooler zone. For a gas grill, light one side to high heat and the other to medium heat. For a charcoal grill, pile hot coals on one side.

3. Add steak to hot side of grill, and cover. Grill 5 minutes; flip, and cook 5 minutes. Move steak to cooler side of grill, and cover. Cook 10 to 15 minutes or until steak reaches desired doneness, 120°F for rare and 130°F for medium-rare (the internal temperature will increase as the steak rests). Transfer steak to a cutting board, tent with foil, and let rest 15 minutes.

4. Meanwhile, toss together onion, oil, and a couple large pinches of salt in a bowl. While the steak rests, place onion on hot side of grill, and cook until tender, about 5 minutes on each side. Remove from grill.

5. Drizzle cut sides of rolls with desired amount of oil, and place cut sides down on hot side of grill. Cover, and cook until toasted, about 3 minutes. Flip rolls over, and sprinkle bottom buns with cheese. Cover, and heat until cheese is melted, about 1 minute.

6. Thinly slice steak against the grain. Divide steak and onion among rolls. Top with barbecue sauce.

Chocolaty Date Overnight Oats

The funky, slow-growing Joshua trees in California's eponymous national park look like something from a Dr. Seuss book. On the park's 300 miles of hiking trails, visitors can get up close and personal with the iconic trees, plus scramble over piles of boulders and other rock formations. More adventurous types can work on their climbing, bouldering, or slacklining. To fuel all those activities, a hearty breakfast is in order. These chocolate overnight oats are a great thing to stash in the fridge the night before a park excursion. Skip the sugar and use dates, which grow in the nearby Coachella Valley.

YIELD: 1 SERVING
HANDS-ON TIME: 10 MINUTES
TOTAL TIME: 8 HOURS 10 MINUTES, INCLUDING CHILLING

⅓ cup old-fashioned rolled oats

1½ teaspoons chia seeds

1½ teaspoons cocoa powder

⅛ teaspoon ground cinnamon

Pinch of salt

½ cup unsweetened almond or oat milk

2 Medjool dates, pitted and chopped

For serving: blackberries or raspberries; chopped, toasted pistachios or almonds; date syrup, honey, or maple syrup

1. Place oats, chia seeds, cocoa powder, cinnamon, and salt in an 8-ounce jar with a lid. Add lid and shake until oats are coated. Stir in milk and chopped dates until everything is well combined.

2. Cover and refrigerate until oats soften and mixture thickens, at least 8 hours or overnight.

3. Stir before serving (directly from the jar or in a bowl) with desired toppings.

Nighttime at the park

Spruce-Cured Salmon

Salting, drying, pickling, smoking—all these techniques are methods by which the Alutiiq people have preserved salmon leading up to the cold winters. Descendants of the Alutiiq people still call the area around Alaska's Katmai National Park and Preserve home, living off the land in a balanced relationship with nature. This sockeye salmon is cured with citrusy spruce tips, which can be foraged from the towering trees come spring. The 36-hour process creates velvety, flavor-packed fish that's perfect for piling on crackers or bagels.

YIELD: 8 SERVINGS
HANDS-ON TIME: 10 MINUTES
TOTAL TIME: 36 HOURS, INCLUDING CURING

½ cup spruce tips or fresh dill sprigs, roughly chopped

½ cup kosher salt

¼ cup granulated sugar

1 tablespoon lemon zest (from about 2 lemons)

1 tablespoon coarsely cracked peppercorns

2 pounds wild Alaska salmon, skin on (1 side of sockeye salmon or 1 large king salmon fillet)

1. In a medium bowl, combine spruce tips, salt, sugar, lemon zest, and pepper.

2. Place a large piece of plastic wrap on a work surface. Pat salmon dry with paper towels, then place on plastic wrap, skin side up. Coat with half the seasoning mixture, and press firmly to adhere as much as possible.

Flip salmon, and coat with remaining seasoning, again pressing to adhere.

3. Wrap salmon tightly in plastic wrap, using a second or third piece if needed. Transfer salmon to a rimmed baking sheet or baking dish, skin side down. Place another baking sheet or a smaller pan on top, then weigh it down with a few cans.

4. Refrigerate salmon for 36 hours, flipping it every 12 hours. (Salmon will leach liquid, so don't be alarmed if the baking sheet is wet.)

5. After 36 hours, unwrap salmon, rinse under cold water, and pat dry. With a very sharp knife, thinly slice enough salmon on an angle to serve. Tightly wrap any remaining salmon, and refrigerate it for up to a week. If freezing, thinly slice and tightly wrap salmon. Freeze for up to 1 month; let thaw overnight in the fridge before using.

Honey-Rosemary Cedar Plank Salmon

Brooks Camp is Katmai National Park and Preserve's most popular destination by far, as visitors head there to catch a glimpse of the famous local brown bears in their natural habitat. An estimated 2,200 brown bears live in the park, outnumbering the human population on the Alaska Peninsula. Situated at the mouth of the Brooks River and the shore of Naknek Lake, Brooks Camp attracts the bears during the sockeye salmon run every summer. This recipe—featuring another bear favorite, honey—is an ode to the brown bears, which are known to eat up to 90 pounds of food per day to prepare for months of hibernation.

YIELD: 4 SERVINGS
HANDS-ON TIME: 20 MINUTES
TOTAL TIME: 3 HOURS, INCLUDING MARINATING AND STANDING

4 cedar planks

2 cloves garlic, chopped

1 lemon, zested and quartered

3 tablespoons olive oil

2 tablespoons honey

2 teaspoons chopped fresh rosemary leaves

2 teaspoons Dijon mustard

1½ teaspoons kosher salt

½ teaspoon pepper

4 (6-ounce) center-cut salmon fillets, skins removed

1. Cover cedar planks in water and let soak. Meanwhile, in a large bowl, whisk together garlic, lemon zest, oil, honey, rosemary, Dijon, salt, and pepper until well combined. Add salmon, turning a few times to coat. Cover bowl with plastic wrap, refrigerate, and marinate for 2 hours. (Alternatively, transfer salmon and marinade to a large zip-top plastic bag.)

2. Remove salmon from fridge, and let stand 30 minutes. Preheat grill to medium-high heat (400°F).

3. Pat cedar planks with paper towels to remove excess water. Place 1 salmon fillet and 1 lemon quarter on each plank. Drizzle salmon with any marinade remaining in bowl.

4. Grill salmon, with lid closed, until fish reaches desired doneness, 10 to 15 minutes. Remove from grill, cool 3 to 4 minutes, then transfer fish and lemon quarters to plates.

Fishing in the Bay of Islands

Kenai Fjords National Park

The Harding Icefield, part of a sweeping ice sheet that covered much of southcentral Alaska more than 23,000 years ago, now spans 700 square miles of Kenai Fjords.

Herb-Butter Halibut With Romesco

Pacific halibut is one of the most prized catches in the waters surrounding Alaska's Kenai Fjords National Park. The fish spawn in the cold, deep ocean during the winter and are most catchable in the summer months when the temperature increases and the fish become more active. At Kenai Fjords Glacier Lodge, located within the park on an Alaska Native–owned wilderness sanctuary, halibut is a mainstay on the restaurant's menu. How the fish is prepared changes regularly—this iteration spent some time on the menu under chef Marisa Kate Gollus—but the view of Pedersen Glacier through the floor-to-ceiling dining room windows is a constant.

YIELD: 4 SERVINGS
HANDS-ON TIME: 35 MINUTES
TOTAL TIME: 35 MINUTES

ROMESCO

¾ cup jarred or fresh roasted red peppers

⅓ cup almonds or sunflower seeds, toasted

⅓ cup packed fresh basil leaves

2 cloves garlic

1 tablespoon tomato paste

1 lemon, zested and halved

¾ teaspoon kosher salt

¼ teaspoon smoked paprika

Pinch of crushed red pepper

2 tablespoons extra-virgin olive oil

HALIBUT

4 Pacific halibut fillets (about 2 pounds)

Kosher salt and black pepper

2 tablespoons vegetable oil

½ cup (1 stick) unsalted butter, sliced

4 sprigs fresh thyme, plus more for garnish

Gentle falls in Kenai Fjords

1. To make the romesco, combine roasted red peppers, almonds, basil, garlic, tomato paste, lemon zest, salt, smoked paprika, and crushed red pepper in a food processor or blender; add juice from half of lemon. Pulse until combined. With processor running, gradually add oil through food chute, and blend until smooth. Taste and add more lemon juice or salt, if needed.

2. To make the halibut, pat fish dry on both sides, and season generously with salt and pepper.

3. Heat oil in a large cast-iron or nonstick skillet over high heat. Once oil is shimmering, place fish in skillet, skin sides up. Cook until flesh is golden brown, about 3 minutes. Flip fish, and reduce heat to medium. Add butter and thyme. Cook until fish is opaque, 3 to 4 minutes more, basting with melted butter.

4. Spoon romesco onto plates, and top with fish and herb-butter sauce. Garnish with thyme.

Adventure Cookies

Cookbook author and food editor Kristine Kidd fell in love with the High Sierras for the dramatic topography, the tight-knit community that lives just outside California's Kings Canyon National Park, and the hiking—and she has her hiking menu locked in. When she and her husband, Steve, stop on the trail for lunch, that menu includes sandwiches made on Lots of Seeds & Nuts Bread (page 158) and these fruit-and-nut-packed cookies. Kidd follows a gluten-free diet, but if you don't, you can make the cookies with the same quantity of all-purpose flour (and omit the xanthan gum).

YIELD: 1 DOZEN COOKIES
HANDS-ON TIME: 20 MINUTES
TOTAL TIME: 2 HOURS 45 MINUTES, INCLUDING CHILLING

½ cup (45 grams) gluten-free rolled oats

½ cup roasted almonds, coarsely chopped

½ cup walnuts or peanuts, coarsely chopped

½ cup pepitas

¾ cup dried tart Montmorency cherries, coarsely chopped

4 ounces bittersweet chocolate from a baking bar, coarsely chopped

¼ cup (½ stick) unsalted butter, melted

⅓ cup (55 grams) packed brown sugar

1 large egg

2 teaspoons vanilla extract

1 teaspoon coarse kosher salt

½ teaspoon baking soda

½ cup (60 grams) gluten-free flour or ½ cup (55 grams) almond flour

Pinch of xanthan gum, if using gluten-free flour

Along Bullfrog Lake and Rae Lakes Loop

1. Preheat oven to 350°F. Place oats on a small pan, and toast until golden brown, stirring once, about 10 minutes. Cool.

2. In a large bowl, toss together cooled oats, almonds, walnuts, pepitas, cherries, and chocolate. Meanwhile, in a medium bowl, whisk together butter, brown sugar, egg, vanilla, salt, and baking soda until blended; stir in flour and xanthan gum, if using. Add to nut mixture, and stir until evenly coated. (There will not be a lot of batter coating the nut mixture, but the dough will firm up as it chills.) Cover and refrigerate for at least 2 hours or up to 3 days.

3. Arrange one rack in upper third and one rack in lower third of oven; preheat to 350°F. Line 2 baking sheets with parchment paper. Scoop 6 scant ⅓ cupfuls of batter, packing firmly, onto each baking sheet (tapping the measuring cup on the baking sheet can help release the batter from the cup). Using damp fingers, press dough into ¾-inch-thick rounds, about 2½ inches in diameter.

4. Bake cookies until golden brown, about 14 minutes, reversing the sheets about halfway through. Let stand on baking sheets until cool enough to handle. Store in an airtight container at room temperature for up to a week, or freeze for up to 3 months.

Lots of Seeds & Nuts Bread

One of the best ways to experience California's Kings Canyon National Park is via the trails that wind in and out of canyons and forests and past impossibly blue alpine lakes. Cookbook author and food editor Kristine Kidd, who lives near the park, can attest to the joys of hiking and camping in this remarkable landscape. She also makes sure her hiking provisions are top-notch. Kidd uses this seed-and-nut-packed gluten-free bread to make open-faced sandwiches—one slice of toasted bread, mayo, mustard, cheese, and a romaine leaf on top—but toasted slices with butter are also super tasty.

YIELD: 1 LOAF

HANDS-ON TIME: 30 MINUTES

TOTAL TIME: 13 HOURS 20 MINUTES, INCLUDING CHILLING, STANDING, RISING, AND COOLING

1¼ cups (300 milliliters) dairy or nondairy milk of choice

1 tablespoon apple cider vinegar

¾ cup (135 grams) gluten-free steel-cut oats

1 cup (120 grams) buckwheat flour

½ cup (65 grams) hemp hearts

¼ cup (30 grams) flaxseed meal

¼ cup (25 grams) whole unflavored psyllium husk

2 tablespoons chia seeds

2 teaspoons kosher salt

½ teaspoon xanthan gum

½ cup roasted pepitas

½ cup sunflower seeds

½ cup roasted almonds, coarsely chopped

½ cup walnuts, coarsely chopped

1 cup hot water (100°F to 110°F)

3 tablespoons maple syrup

1 teaspoon instant or active dry yeast

¼ cup extra-virgin olive oil

1. In a small bowl, stir milk and vinegar until blended. Mix in oats. Cover and refrigerate until oats soften and mixture thickens, at least 8 hours or overnight.

2. In a large bowl, stir together buckwheat flour, hemp hearts, flaxseed meal, psyllium husk, chia seeds, salt, and xanthan gum until blended. Mix in pepitas, sunflower seeds, almonds, and walnuts.

3. In a large liquid measuring cup, combine hot water and maple syrup. Sprinkle yeast over water, and mix. Let stand until mixture begins to foam and is fragrant, about 5 minutes. Add to dry ingredients. Stir in oat mixture and olive oil until well blended. (The dough will seem thin at first but will thicken as you stir it.)

4. Cover bowl with plastic wrap, and let dough rise in a warm area until slightly puffy and less dense (it will not rise as high as other breads), 1 hour 15 minutes to 1 hour 30 minutes.

5. Line a loaf pan with parchment paper. Stir dough to deflate. Add dough to loaf pan, smoothing the surface slightly. Cover with plastic wrap, and let rise in a warm area until puffy and slightly domed, 1 hour to 1 hour 15 minutes.

6. Preheat oven to 350°F. Remove plastic wrap from pan, and bake until bread is dark brown and firm to the touch and an instant-read thermometer inserted into center registers 190°F to 200°F, about 1 hour 20 minutes.

7. Transfer pan to a wire rack, and let bread cool for 10 minutes. Turn bread out onto rack, remove parchment if stuck to bread, and cool completely before slicing, about 1 hour. Wrap bread airtight and store in refrigerator for up to 2 weeks. If freezing, wrap tightly in plastic wrap, followed by a layer of aluminum foil. Freeze for up to 3 months; thaw at room temperature.

Caribou Soup

Twice each year, the Western Arctic caribou herd crosses the Kobuk River near the Onion Portage in Alaska's Kobuk Valley National Park. The herd is hundreds of thousands of caribou deep, and locals have depended on them as a primary source of food for thousands of years. The herd size has dropped drastically in the last 25 years due to both hunting and climate change, but recent reports show caribou are on the rebound. This soup is a classic preparation in the Kobuk Valley and can be adapted to whatever vegetables a cook has on hand—just be sure to simmer it low and slow to keep the lean meat tender.

YIELD: 6 SERVINGS
HANDS-ON TIME: 35 MINUTES
TOTAL TIME: 1 HOUR 45 MINUTES

1 pound caribou or venison stew meat

2 teaspoons kosher salt, divided, plus more for seasoning

½ teaspoon pepper

2 tablespoons vegetable oil, divided

2 large carrots, cut into ½-inch-thick pieces

2 large stalks celery, diced

1 medium onion, diced

4 large cloves garlic, chopped

1 sprig fresh rosemary or ½ teaspoon dried

1 tablespoon tomato paste

½ cup dry red wine or water

1 quart beef stock or broth

2 cups water

1 large russet potato (about 12 ounces)

1 cup uncooked large elbow noodles

1 tablespoon Worcestershire sauce

Chopped fresh parsley (optional)

Ahnewetut Creek

1. Pat caribou dry with paper towels. Dice into ¾-inch cubes. Transfer to a medium bowl, and season with 1 teaspoon salt and pepper.

2. Heat a large Dutch oven or heavy-bottomed pot over medium-high heat. Add 1 tablespoon oil, then add caribou in an even layer. Cook, stirring once about halfway through, until browned, about 4 minutes. Transfer to a plate with a slotted spoon.

3. Add remaining 1 tablespoon oil to pot. Stir in carrots, celery, and onion. Cook, stirring occasionally, until just starting to soften, 3 to 5 minutes. Stir in garlic and rosemary; cook for 1 minute. Stir in tomato paste; cook for 1 minute.

4. Pour in wine. Cook, stirring and scraping bottom of pot to release any browned bits. Simmer for 1 minute. Return caribou to pot and add beef stock, 2 cups water, and remaining 1 teaspoon salt. Bring to a boil, then reduce heat to low, cover, and simmer until caribou is tender, about 45 minutes.

5. Peel potato, and dice into 1-inch cubes. Stir into soup, and return to a simmer; cook for 10 minutes. Stir in pasta, and cook until tender, about 10 minutes. Stir in Worcestershire. Taste, and season with salt and pepper, if needed.

6. Sprinkle each serving with parsley, if desired. Store leftovers in an airtight container in the refrigerator for up to 4 days, or freeze for up to 3 months.

Smoked Sockeye Salmon Grain Salad

The "fish basket" of Bristol Bay, located on the eastern edge of the Bering Sea in southwestern Alaska, is the epicenter of the world's largest wild salmon run. Lake Clark is pivotal to the sockeye (or red) salmon's success—the fish swim upstream from Bristol Bay to spawn in the fresh waters of Lake Clark National Park and Preserve. Come summer, the salmon are abundant and become a prized catch. The lean fish holds up well to hot smoking, resulting in a deeply flavorful and flaky fish that can be served alongside scrambled eggs, added to a creamy chowder, or tossed in a salad.

YIELD: 4 SERVINGS

HANDS-ON TIME: 15 MINUTES

TOTAL TIME: 30 MINUTES

1½ cups quick-cooking farro

1 lemon, zested and juiced

3 tablespoons balsamic vinegar

2 teaspoons Dijon mustard

5 tablespoons extra-virgin olive oil

½ small shallot, minced

¾ teaspoon kosher salt, plus more for seasoning

¼ teaspoon pepper, plus more for seasoning

¾ cup sweetened dried cranberries

½ cup fresh parsley leaves and tender stems, chopped

⅓ cup chopped toasted walnuts

4 ounces hot smoked salmon, flaked

1. In a medium pot, cook farro in salted water according to package directions. Drain in a fine-mesh strainer, and rinse under cold water for 1 minute to stop the cooking process; drain well again.

2. Meanwhile, in a medium bowl, whisk together lemon zest and juice, vinegar, and Dijon. Gradually add olive oil in a steady stream, whisking until well blended. Whisk in shallot, salt, and pepper.

3. Add farro to dressing, along with cranberries, parsley, and walnuts; mix until combined. Season with more salt and pepper, if necessary. Gently fold in salmon.

4. Serve at room temperature or chilled. Store in an airtight container in the refrigerator for up to 2 days.

The original Twin Lakes Ranger Station cabin in 1983

Ranch Rib Eyes

Nestled below the Cascade mountain range, Drakesbad Guest Ranch in California's Lassen Volcanic National Park offers a remote getaway for travelers looking to get off the grid. Edward R. Drake, an early settler, arrived in the Warner Valley sometime around 1875, eventually purchasing the land where the lodge now sits. He built some facilities, including a large log cabin—the present-day guest ranch—to host occasional campers. In 1900, Drake sold the land to the Sifford family, who continued hosting visitors. The Siffords began raising cattle in 1942 as a response to the meat shortage during World War II, a practice they continued until the ranch was sold to the National Park Service about a decade later.

YIELD: 4 SERVINGS
HANDS-ON TIME: 20 MINUTES
TOTAL TIME: 55 MINUTES, INCLUDING STANDING

2 (1½-pound) bone-in rib eye steaks (about 1½ inches thick)

Kosher salt

Pepper

1 tablespoon vegetable oil

3 tablespoons butter

4 large cloves garlic

3 sprigs fresh thyme

2 sprigs fresh rosemary

Flaky salt (optional)

1. Pat steaks dry with paper towels. Season generously all over with kosher salt, and let stand on a baking sheet fitted with a wire rack for 30 minutes to 1 hour.

2. Heat a large cast-iron skillet over medium-high heat. Pat steaks dry with paper towels, then season both sides with pepper. Heat oil in skillet, then add steaks. Cook until browned, 5 to 6 minutes. Flip steaks, and add butter, garlic, thyme, and rosemary to skillet. Cook, basting steaks frequently with melted butter, until medium-rare, 5 to 6 minutes.

3. Transfer steaks to a cutting board to stand 5 minutes, then slice steaks against the grain. Serve family style on a platter with garlic, herbs, and any butter from pan. Sprinkle with flaky salt, if desired.

Appalachian Spoon Bread

Mammoth Cave National Park is the world's longest known cave system, with more than 400 miles of passageways. But above the labyrinth of stalactites and stalagmites is the lush Green River Valley, with its rolling hills and deciduous forests. In this part of Kentucky, you'll find a subset of southern cuisine aptly named Appalachian after the idyllic mountain range, which features locally sourced ingredients like morel mushrooms, ramps, and rabbit. Corn, in all its forms, is one of the hallmarks of Appalachian cooking, and this pudding-like spoon bread speaks to the region's comforting cuisine.

YIELD: 6 TO 8 SERVINGS
HANDS-ON TIME: 30 MINUTES
TOTAL TIME: 1 HOUR 25 MINUTES, INCLUDING COOLING

¼ cup (½ stick) unsalted butter, cut into pieces, plus more for greasing pan and serving

3½ cups (840 milliliters) milk

1 cup (155 grams) fine- or medium-grain yellow cornmeal

1½ teaspoons kosher salt

3 large eggs, separated

1 tablespoon granulated sugar

¼ teaspoon cream of tartar

Honey (optional)

The Frozen Niagara section

1. Preheat oven to 400°F. Generously grease a 3-inch-deep (1½- to 2-quart) soufflé or baking dish with butter. (If you use a 1½-quart dish, the spoon bread will rise up more dramatically, but the dish will be filled to the brim. Place the dish on a baking sheet to catch any possible overflow in the oven.)

2. In a large skillet, heat milk over medium heat until gently bubbling. Slowly pour in cornmeal, whisking constantly, and return to a simmer. Reduce heat to medium-low, and simmer until thickened, stirring frequently, 1 to 5 minutes, depending on cornmeal used (fine-grain thickens quicker). Remove skillet from heat, then whisk in butter and salt. Cool for 10 minutes, stirring occasionally to prevent a skin from forming.

3. In a medium bowl, whisk egg yolks and sugar until pale yellow, about 2 minutes. In another medium bowl, using an electric mixer, beat egg whites and cream of tartar at medium speed until frothy, about 1 minute. Increase speed to medium-high, and beat until stiff peaks form, about 2 minutes.

4. Vigorously whisk egg yolk mixture into cooled cornmeal. Gently fold in egg whites until just combined. Transfer mixture to prepared soufflé dish, and smooth top.

5. Place in oven, and immediately reduce heat to 350°F. Bake until spoon bread is puffed and golden brown (it will still be jiggly, and the inside will be creamy, similar to a soufflé), 45 to 55 minutes.

6. Serve immediately with butter and honey, if desired.

Kentucky Burgoo

The forests and rolling hills of Mammoth Cave National Park might not be the park's biggest draw, but they are a must-visit. They're packed with wildlife—and some of that game continues to be a food source for locals. This Appalachian stew, traditionally simmered for hours in a large cast-iron pot set over a fire, is a Kentucky classic. It has historically included wild game native to the area, such as white-tailed deer and eastern gray squirrel. This recipe uses more readily available meats that you'll find at the store, similar to the burgoo made in many homes today.

YIELD: 8 SERVINGS
HANDS-ON TIME: 1 HOUR
TOTAL TIME: 2 HOURS 45 MINUTES

2 skin-on, bone-in chicken thighs (about 1½ pounds)

Kosher salt

Black pepper

2 to 3 tablespoons vegetable oil, divided

1 pound beef chuck roast or lamb shoulder or leg, cut into 1½-inch cubes

1 pound boneless pork shoulder, cut into 1½-inch cubes

3 stalks celery, diced

2 large carrots, diced

1 large green bell pepper, diced

1 medium yellow onion, diced

4 large cloves garlic, chopped

2 tablespoons tomato paste

1 (14.5-ounce) can diced tomatoes

1 quart chicken stock or broth

2 russet potatoes (about 1 pound)

2 cups frozen lima beans

2 cups sliced (½-inch thick) fresh or frozen cut okra (optional)

1½ cups fresh (about 2 ears) or frozen corn kernels

2 tablespoons Worcestershire sauce

Hot sauce (optional)

1. Pat chicken thighs dry with paper towels. Season on both sides with salt and pepper. Heat 1 tablespoon oil in a large Dutch oven or heavy-bottomed pot over medium-high heat. Add chicken, skin sides down, and cook until skin is golden and releases easily from pot, about 3 minutes. Flip and cook 2 minutes more, then transfer to a large plate or bowl.

2. Season beef cubes all over with salt and pepper, then add to pot. Cook until browned on one side, about 2 minutes; turn and cook 2 minutes more. Transfer to plate with chicken.

3. Season pork all over with salt and pepper. If needed, add 1 tablespoon oil to pot, then add pork. Cook until browned on one side, about 2 minutes; turn and cook 2 minutes more. Transfer to plate with chicken and beef.

4. Add remaining 1 tablespoon oil to pot. Stir in celery, carrots, bell pepper, onion, and garlic.

Add 1 teaspoon salt and ½ teaspoon pepper. Cook, stirring occasionally, until vegetables start to soften, about 5 minutes. Stir in tomato paste until everything is coated; cook 1 minute.

5. Pour in diced tomatoes. Bring to a simmer, scraping bottom of pot to release any browned bits. Pour in stock, and add 1 teaspoon salt. Stir in chicken, beef, and pork. Bring to a boil, then reduce heat to low, cover, and cook at a consistent low simmer for 1 hour 15 minutes.

6. Using tongs, transfer chicken to a cutting board; let cool slightly. Peel potatoes, and cut into 1-inch cubes; stir into pot. Shred chicken with a fork, discarding skin and bones; stir meat into pot. Return stew to a simmer, and cook until meat and potatoes are fork-tender, about 20 minutes.

7. Stir lima beans, okra (if using), and corn into stew. Return to a simmer, increasing heat slightly if necessary; cook until beans are tender, about 10 minutes. Stir in Worcestershire, then season with salt and pepper.

8. Serve with hot sauce, if desired. Store leftovers in an airtight container in the refrigerator for up to 3 days, or freeze for up to 3 months.

Chicken Tortilla Soup

About 15 miles past the entrance into Mesa Verde National Park, visitors will find Far View Lodge, the only hotel within the park. It's a cozy home base for exploring, whether that's via hiking, stargazing, or admiring the incredible cliff dwellings. The southwestern Colorado park is also a great place to visit in the winter. When there's enough snow, visitors can cross-country ski or snowshoe on groomed trails. A bowl of chicken tortilla soup, like this one inspired by the version served at the lodge's Metate Room, is a great way to warm up après-ski.

YIELD: 6 TO 8 SERVINGS
HANDS-ON TIME: 25 MINUTES
TOTAL TIME: 50 MINUTES

2 tablespoons vegetable oil

1 medium white or yellow onion, diced

4 large cloves garlic, chopped

1 (28-ounce) can crushed tomatoes

1 (4-ounce) can diced green chiles

1 quart chicken stock

3 cups shredded cooked chicken

1 (15-ounce) can black beans, drained and rinsed

1 cup fresh or frozen corn kernels

1 cup fresh cilantro leaves and tender stems, chopped, plus more for serving

1 teaspoon kosher salt

½ teaspoon pepper

½ cup crushed tortilla strips or chips, plus more strips for serving

2 limes, halved

For serving: crema or sour cream, shredded Monterey Jack cheese, diced avocado, sliced jalapeño peppers

1. In a large Dutch oven or pot, heat oil over medium-high heat. Add onion and garlic. Cook, stirring occasionally, until softened, 3 to 5 minutes. Add tomatoes, chiles, and stock. Bring to a simmer; cook for 5 minutes.

2. Stir in chicken, beans, corn, and cilantro. Add salt and pepper. Return to a simmer, then reduce heat to medium-low. Simmer, uncovered and stirring occasionally, for 20 minutes.

3. Stir in tortilla strips and juice from 1 lime. Simmer until soup has slightly thickened, 2 to 3 minutes. Season with salt and pepper to taste. Cut remaining lime into wedges. Serve soup with lime wedges, desired toppings, and additional cilantro and tortilla strips.

Cliff Palace

Lemon Tres Leches Cake

The incredible ancestral Puebloan cliff dwellings are the main draw at Colorado's Mesa Verde National Park. The sandstone structures, some of which are estimated to have been built between 1190 and 1280 C.E., speak to the engineering and artistic talents of the people who once called what became known as Mesa Verde home. Today's visitors can take guided tours of the structures and then reflect on the engineering marvel over dinner at the Far View Lodge's Metate Room inside the park. For dessert, diners can order the supermoist, citrus-infused cake that inspired the recipe here.

YIELD: 12 SERVINGS
HANDS-ON TIME: 35 MINUTES
TOTAL TIME: 9 HOURS 30 MINUTES, INCLUDING COOLING AND CHILLING

CAKE

Butter, for greasing pan

1½ cups (180 grams) all-purpose flour

2 teaspoons baking powder

½ teaspoon kosher salt

5 large eggs, at room temperature and separated

1 cup (200 grams) granulated sugar

½ cup (120 milliliters) whole milk or heavy cream

2 large lemons, zested and juiced

1½ teaspoons vanilla extract

1 teaspoon cream of tartar

TRES LECHES MIXTURE

1 (14-ounce) can sweetened condensed milk

1 (12-ounce) can evaporated milk

½ cup (120 milliliters) whole milk or heavy cream

TOPPING

2 cups (480 milliliters) heavy cream, chilled

3 tablespoons granulated sugar

2 teaspoons lemon zest

1 teaspoon vanilla extract

Sliced lemons and lemon zest (optional)

1. Preheat oven to 350°F. Grease a 9-by-13-inch baking dish with butter.

2. In a medium bowl, whisk together flour, baking powder, and salt. In a large bowl, combine egg yolks and sugar. Using an electric mixer, beat on medium-high speed until thick and pale yellow, 1 to 2 minutes. Beat in

whole milk, lemon zest and juice, and vanilla until just combined. Add flour mixture, and beat until just combined.

3. Clean the beaters. In a separate large bowl, beat egg whites and cream of tartar on medium-low speed until frothy, then increase speed to medium-high, and beat until stiff peaks form, 4 to 5 minutes.

4. Gently fold egg whites into flour mixture until just combined. (Do not overmix.) Transfer batter into prepared baking dish.

5. Bake until cake is golden and a toothpick inserted into the center comes out clean, about 25 minutes. Cool completely.

6. Use a paring knife to loosen the cooled cake from sides of baking dish. Use a wooden skewer to poke holes all over surface. To make the tres leches mixture, in a medium bowl, whisk together the sweetened condensed milk, evaporated milk, and whole milk. Slowly pour mixture evenly over cake; it will pool at first but will eventually soak into the cake. Cover, and refrigerate at least 8 hours or, preferably, overnight.

7. To make the topping, in a large metal bowl, beat heavy cream, sugar, lemon zest, and vanilla at medium-high speed until nearly stiff peaks form, about 4 minutes. Spread evenly over cake. If desired, sprinkle cake with lemon zest and garnish with sliced lemons. Serve immediately, or chill up to 2 hours before serving.

Buffalo Meatloaf (page 176)
and Whiskey Glaze (page 177)

Buffalo Meatloaf

Mount Rainier, the 14,410-foot active volcano, is at the heart of this national park in Washington State. Visitors can take a leisurely hike and admire the peak from a distance, road-trip around the mountain, or (with the proper training, fees, and permits) climb to the summit. When you're finished with your own Mount Rainier adventure, stop by the National Park Inn for dinner, where you can order this tender bison meatloaf.

YIELD: 8 SERVINGS
HANDS-ON TIME: 30 MINUTES
TOTAL TIME: 1 HOUR 25 MINUTES, NOT INCLUDING GLAZE

2 tablespoons olive oil

2 stalks celery, finely chopped

1 large carrot, finely chopped

1 small onion, finely chopped

2 cloves garlic, finely chopped

2 teaspoons ground cumin

2 tablespoons tomato paste

1 tablespoon lemon juice

2 tablespoons ketchup

1 tablespoon Worcestershire sauce

1 teaspoon dried parsley

1 cup old-fashioned oats

1 pound ground bison

½ pound ground beef

½ pound ground pork

2 large eggs, beaten

1 teaspoon kosher salt

½ teaspoon pepper

Whiskey Glaze (optional; at right)

1. Preheat oven to 350°F. In a large skillet, heat oil over medium heat. Add celery, carrot, and onion. Cook, stirring frequently, until vegetables soften, 6 to 8 minutes. Add garlic, and cook until fragrant, about 1 minute. Add cumin, and stir until fragrant, about 30 seconds. Add tomato paste, and stir until slightly browned, about 1 minute. Stir in lemon juice, scraping up any browned bits on bottom of skillet. Stir in ketchup, Worcestershire, and parsley. Remove from heat.

2. In a food processor, pulse oats until ground.

3. In a large bowl, mix together oats, bison, beef, pork, eggs, salt, and pepper until just combined. Add cooled vegetable mixture, and mix until just combined (do not overmix). Transfer meatloaf mixture to a loaf pan. Place on a baking sheet lined with foil to catch any drips.

4. Bake until a meat thermometer inserted into center registers 155°F to 160°F, 45 minutes to 1 hour. Brush liberally with Whiskey Glaze, if desired. Let stand 10 minutes before slicing.

Whiskey Glaze

Meatloaf is good, but meatloaf with glaze is better. The bison meatloaf that's served at Mount Rainier's National Park Inn in Washington State is brushed with a generous amount of this whiskey-spiked sauce, taking the classic comfort dish up a notch (or three). The savory-sweet combination of teriyaki sauce, soy sauce, brown sugar, and garlic is the perfect finishing touch. Any leftovers are great for brushing on burgers, ribs, or chicken.

YIELD: 1¾ CUPS
HANDS-ON TIME: 15 MINUTES
TOTAL TIME: 1 HOUR 30 MINUTES, INCLUDING COOLING

---

1 head garlic

1 tablespoon olive oil, plus more for drizzling

1⅓ cups packed dark brown sugar

1 cup pineapple juice

⅔ cup water

¼ cup teriyaki sauce

3 tablespoons minced white onion

3 tablespoons lemon juice

1 tablespoon soy sauce

1 tablespoon bourbon whiskey

1 tablespoon crushed pineapple

¼ teaspoon cayenne pepper

1. Preheat oven to 400°F. Remove outermost papery layers from garlic (just a few layers; you want the head to stay intact). Cut just enough off the top of the head to expose the cloves. Place garlic on a piece of aluminum foil. Drizzle exposed cloves with oil, wrap in foil, and roast until cloves are lightly brown and very tender, 30 to 40 minutes. Let stand until cool enough to touch.

2. Using a small sharp knife, remove cloves from papery skin, or squeeze cloves out into a saucepan.

3. Add 1 tablespoon oil and remaining ingredients to pan. Bring to a simmer over medium heat. Reduce heat to low, and simmer, stirring frequently, until sauce thickens and coats the back of a spoon, 30 to 40 minutes.

Fried Green Tomatoes

Despite its name, New River Gorge National Park and Preserve in West Virginia features one of the oldest rivers on the continent. What *is* newer is the national park designation, which became official in 2020. Whether you've spent the day climbing the sandstone cliffs, hiking the backcountry, or whitewater rafting, a delicious meal is in order. The Tamarack Marketplace, just down the road from the park, serves up Appalachian specialties, including these fried green tomatoes. There, you can even order a fried green tomato breakfast sandwich with applewood smoked bacon and eggs, then pick up some local art in the adjacent gallery, which has rotating exhibits.

YIELD: 4 TO 6 SERVINGS

HANDS-ON TIME: 40 MINUTES

TOTAL TIME: 40 MINUTES

Vegetable oil, for frying (about 4 cups)

3 large unripe green tomatoes

1¾ cups all-purpose flour

2 tablespoons garlic powder

2 tablespoons Cajun seasoning

3 teaspoons kosher salt

1 teaspoon pepper

1½ cups buttermilk

1 cup fine-grain cornmeal

Thousand Island dressing (optional)

The New River Gorge

1. Pour 1 inch oil into a large Dutch oven or heavy-bottomed pot. Heat over medium-high heat until a deep-fry thermometer registers 350°F. Line a baking sheet with parchment paper. Line a second baking sheet with paper towels.

2. Cut tomatoes into ¼-inch-thick slices.

3. In a bowl, combine 1 cup flour, 1 tablespoon garlic powder, 1 tablespoon Cajun seasoning, 1½ teaspoons salt, and ½ teaspoon pepper. In another bowl, add buttermilk. In a third bowl, combine cornmeal and remaining ¾ cup flour, 1 tablespoon garlic powder, 1 tablespoon Cajun seasoning, 1½ teaspoons salt, and ½ teaspoon pepper.

4. One at a time, coat tomato slices in flour mixture, shaking off excess. Dip in buttermilk, turning to coat. Coat in cornmeal mixture. Place slices in a single layer on parchment-lined baking sheet.

5. Fry tomatoes in batches, being careful not to overcrowd the pot, until golden brown, about 3 to 4 minutes, adjusting the heat as necessary to maintain the temperature of the oil. Transfer fried tomatoes to paper towels.

6. Serve immediately with Thousand Island dressing, if desired.

Almost There Poutine

The Stehekin Valley has long been a passageway for travelers, linking Washington State's interior wilderness to the Cascade Range. Appropriately, the name Stehekin stems from a Native American Salishan word meaning "the way through." Because the Lodge at Stehekin, situated along the shore of Lake Chelan (the third deepest lake in the United States), is connected to the outside world only by foot, boat, or plane, life is a little slower there. At the lodge's restaurant, visitors can order the Almost There Poutine—rosemary fries topped with braised beef and beer cheese. As they say at the restaurant, "You're not quite to Canada, and this isn't quite poutine."

YIELD: 6 TO 8 SERVINGS
HANDS-ON TIME: 40 MINUTES
TOTAL TIME: 3 HOURS 40 MINUTES

BRAISED BEEF

3 to 4 pounds beef chuck roast, cut into 3-inch pieces

1 tablespoon kosher salt, plus more for seasoning

1½ teaspoons pepper

1 teaspoon ground cumin

3 tablespoons vegetable oil, plus more if needed

1 yellow onion, quartered

2 jalapeño peppers, halved (seeded, if desired)

6 cloves garlic, crushed

¼ cup tomato paste

1½ cups amber beer

5 cups beef stock

½ cup chopped fresh cilantro

1 lime, halved

FRIES

1 (16-ounce) package frozen french fries

2 teaspoons finely chopped fresh rosemary leaves

BEER CHEESE

2 teaspoons vegetable oil

¼ cup pico de gallo

1 teaspoon ground cumin

1 cup whole milk

1 pound white American cheese, cut into small cubes

3 tablespoons amber beer

Kosher salt

For serving: sweet-hot pickled peppers or peppadew peppers, crumbled feta cheese, chopped fresh cilantro, chopped green onions

1. To make the braised beef, season beef with salt, pepper, and cumin. Heat oil in a large, heavy-bottomed pot over medium heat. Cook beef in

batches in hot oil until browned on all sides, about 4 to 5 minutes per batch (add more oil between batches, if needed). Transfer beef to a plate.

from bottom of pot. Add stock and cilantro. Bring to a simmer, cover, then reduce heat to low. Simmer until the beef is fork-tender, about 3 hours.

4. Discard any fat left in the pot, then transfer beef to a plate using a slotted spoon, reserving vegetables in pot. Using an immersion blender, blend liquid and vegetables until smooth. (Alternatively, carefully transfer liquid and vegetables to a regular blender, and process until smooth.)

5. Return vegetable mixture to pot, and season with salt and lime juice to taste. Return beef to pot. (You can make the beef up to 1 day ahead.)

6. To make the fries, prepare according to package directions. Toss with rosemary while hot.

7. To make the beer cheese, heat oil in a medium saucepan over medium heat. Add pico de gallo and cumin; cook, stirring often, until pico de gallo is softened and cumin is fragrant, about 2 minutes.

8. Reduce heat to medium-low, and add milk. Cook, stirring often, until milk just begins to steam, about 2 minutes. Add cheese in batches, stirring until it's completely melted after each addition. Stir in enough beer to reach desired consistency. Season with salt, if needed.

9. Arrange fries on a large plate or platter. Top with braised beef and juices, beer cheese, and desired toppings.

2. Add onion, jalapeños, and garlic to pot. Cook, stirring occasionally, until softened and onion is golden, 5 minutes. Stir in tomato paste, and cook until deepened in color and aroma, about 1 minute.

3. Return beef to pot. Add beer, scraping up any browned bits

Olympic National Park

Built in 1952, Hurricane Ridge Day Lodge was nestled amid the trees of the Bailey Range. The lodge served as a visitors center until it burned down in 2023. Efforts are under way to rebuild the lodge; the trails around Hurricane Ridge remain open to visitors.

Lake Crescent Clam Chowder

Olympic National Park protects nearly one million acres of Washington State's Olympic Peninsula, including old-growth forests, snowcapped mountains, rivers, and more than 70 miles of Pacific coastline. The historic Lake Crescent Lodge (opened in 1937) offers a restaurant menu that reflects some of the great seafood that can be found on the coast, including Dungeness crab, Pacific cod, and clams. Visitors can harvest multiple types of clams (littleneck, butter, Manila, horse, and razor) in season—or take the easier route and order a cup of the lodge's clam chowder.

YIELD: 6 TO 8 SERVINGS
HANDS-ON TIME: 15 MINUTES
TOTAL TIME: 1 HOUR 10 MINUTES

1 cup (6 ounces) finely chopped uncooked bacon

1 small yellow onion, finely chopped

2 stalks celery, finely chopped

2 cloves garlic, finely chopped

¼ cup dry sherry

1 pound Yukon Gold potatoes, peeled and cut into ⅓-inch cubes

2 (8-ounce) bottles clam juice

Vegetable oil, if needed

¾ cup all-purpose flour

3 cups whole milk

1 teaspoon dried thyme

1 dried bay leaf

3 (6.5-ounce) cans chopped clams with juices

Salt and pepper

Oyster crackers or crusty bread

1. In a large, heavy-bottomed pot, cook bacon over medium-low heat until crispy, stirring occasionally, about 20 minutes. Transfer bacon to a plate, and pour drippings into a heatproof bowl, reserving 1 tablespoon in pot.

2. Increase heat to medium. Add onion, celery, and garlic to pot; cook until softened and onion is lightly browned, stirring occasionally, 4 to 5 minutes. Add sherry, and stir, scraping up browned bits from bottom of pot. Cook until sherry evaporates, about 1 minute.

3. Add potatoes and clam juice. Increase heat to medium-high, and bring mixture to a boil. Reduce heat to medium, and let simmer while you make the roux.

4. In a small saucepan, make a roux by adding enough reserved bacon drippings to equal 6 tablespoons, adding oil if necessary. Whisk in flour, and cook over medium heat, whisking often, until mixture is light golden, about 10 minutes.

5. When potatoes are tender, add milk, thyme, and bay leaf. Increase heat to medium-high, and bring to a boil. Stir in hot roux. Reduce heat to medium, and simmer until thickened.

6. Stir in clams, and cook until heated through, about 1 minute. Season with salt and pepper to taste. Discard bay leaf. Serve with cooked bacon and oyster crackers.

Olympic's coastline at sunset

Chili con Carne (page 188) and
Navajo Tacos (page 189)

Chili con Carne

Petrified Forest is two destinations in one national park: Visitors can explore trails with fossilized wood—some small, some giant, and some studded with crystals. They can also hike or drive through the Painted Desert, colorful badlands in Arizona's high desert. Next to the park's visitors center, the Painted Desert Diner serves up locally inspired comfort food, including this meaty, beany chili. Order a bowl topped with cheddar cheese, or have it served on top of fry bread for a Navajo Taco (at right).

YIELD: 8 SERVINGS

HANDS-ON TIME: 15 MINUTES

TOTAL TIME: 40 MINUTES

1 pound ground beef

¾ teaspoon kosher salt

1 small onion, chopped

1 small green or red bell pepper, chopped

1 tablespoon chili powder

1 teaspoon black pepper

1 teaspoon ground cumin

1 teaspoon garlic powder

2 (15.5-ounce) cans pinto beans, drained

1 (28-ounce) can tomato puree

1 (4-ounce) can mild green chiles, drained

1 teaspoon cornstarch

2 teaspoons water

1. In a large pot or deep skillet, add beef and salt. Cook over medium-high heat, breaking up and stirring often, until meat is browned, about 5 minutes. Transfer meat to a plate, and pour off all but 1 tablespoon drippings.

2. Add onion and bell pepper to pot. Cook, stirring often, until softened, 3 to 4 minutes. Sprinkle spices over vegetables, and cook, stirring often, until toasted, about 1 minute.

3. Return beef to pot, and add beans, tomato puree, and chiles. Stir until blended. Bring chili to a simmer.

4. In a small bowl, whisk together cornstarch and 2 teaspoons water. Drizzle cornstarch mixture over chili, and stir to combine. Let simmer until chili thickens, 5 to 10 minutes.

Navajo Tacos

Fry bread is a foundational recipe, but it's anything but basic. The deep-fried dough is a symbolic food in the Native American community, linked to the Long Walk of the 1860s, when the U.S. government forced the Navajo people from their homeland in Arizona and made them walk to New Mexico. The government gave the Navajo rations, which included lard, flour, water, and salt, the building blocks of fry bread. For some, fry bread is a symbol of intertribal unity; for others, it's a food best left in the past. At the Painted Desert Diner, the Navajo Tacos—fry bread topped with chili—are meant to honor the people of the Navajo Nation.

YIELD: 6 SERVINGS
HANDS-ON TIME: 30 MINUTES
TOTAL TIME: 50 MINUTES, NOT INCLUDING CHILI CON CARNE

2½ cups (300 grams) all-purpose flour

1 tablespoon baking powder

1 teaspoon kosher salt

1 cup lukewarm water

Vegetable oil, for frying

Chili con Carne (at left)

For serving: chopped iceberg lettuce, chopped tomatoes, chopped onions, grated cheddar cheese, sour cream

1. In a large bowl, stir together flour, baking powder, and salt until well combined. Slowly mix in water until dough comes together in a shaggy ball.

2. Turn dough onto a lightly floured surface and knead until smooth, 5 to 8 minutes. Divide into 6 equal balls. Cover with plastic wrap or a kitchen towel, and let stand 20 minutes.

3. Meanwhile, pour oil to a depth of 2 inches into a large pot or deep skillet. Heat oil over medium-high heat until it reaches 350°F. Set a wire rack in a large baking sheet.

4. Roll out each dough ball on a flat surface, and stretch into 6-inch rounds. Tear a small hole in the center of each round to prevent them from puffing up in the middle while frying.

5. Carefully add 1 dough round to hot oil, and fry until golden, 1 to 2 minutes per side. Transfer to wire rack. Repeat with remaining dough.

6. Serve Chili con Carne on fry bread with desired toppings.

Beef Barbacoa Flautas (page 192) and Pomegranate Guacamole (page 193)

Beef Barbacoa Flautas

On your way to or from Pinnacles National Park, you'll likely pass through Soledad, California, a town about 20 minutes from the park that has a beautifully restored mission, a collection of wineries, and several great Mexican restaurants, including Cocuyo's, whose extensive menu makes it a local favorite. Stop there pre- or post-hike and consider ordering the flautas. Cocuyo's serves up a chicken version, but this beef take will keep you fueled for all your Pinnacles adventures.

YIELD: 12 FLAUTAS
HANDS-ON TIME: 1 HOUR
TOTAL TIME: 5 HOURS, INCLUDING SLOW COOKING

1 tablespoon ancho chile powder

1 tablespoon kosher salt

½ teaspoon black pepper

½ teaspoon ground allspice

3 pounds beef chuck roast, cut into 3 large pieces

2 tablespoons vegetable oil, plus more for frying

1 medium white onion, diced

6 large cloves garlic

3 sprigs fresh oregano or 1 teaspoon dried oregano (preferably Mexican)

2 bay leaves

2 canned chipotle chile peppers in adobo sauce, chopped

1 tablespoon apple cider vinegar

¾ cup water

Lime wedges, for serving

12 (8-inch) flour tortillas

For serving: shredded iceberg lettuce, crema or sour cream, pico de gallo, hot sauce, and Pomegranate Guacamole (at right)

1. In a small bowl, combine ancho chile powder, salt, pepper, and allspice. Pat beef dry, and rub all over with spice blend.

2. In a large skillet, heat oil over medium-high heat. Add beef, and cook, turning once, until browned, 2 to 3 minutes per side. Transfer to a plate.

3. Add onion and whole garlic cloves to skillet; cook, stirring occasionally, until starting to soften, 2 to 3 minutes. Stir in oregano and bay leaves; cook 30 seconds. Add chipotle peppers, vinegar, and ¾ cup water. Bring to a simmer, scraping bottom of pan to remove any browned bits. Pour into a slow cooker, then add beef and any accumulated juices. (Or cook everything in a slow cooker if you have one with a sauté function.)

4. Cover and cook on high for 4 to 5 hours or low for 7 to 8 hours, until the beef is fall-apart tender. Transfer beef to a large bowl, and shred with two forks.

5. Transfer remaining ingredients in slow cooker to a blender (including bay leaves). Blend until smooth. Pour ¾ cup sauce over shredded beef, and toss until coated. Adjust seasonings as desired, adding more sauce, a

Recipe Note

Flautas can be made ahead and frozen before frying: Place on a parchment paper–lined baking sheet, and freeze until firm, then cover tightly with plastic wrap, and freeze for up to 3 months. Fry from frozen, adding 1 to 2 minutes to frying time.

squeeze of lime juice, and salt to taste.

6. Pour ½ inch of oil into a large, heavy-bottomed skillet. Heat over medium-high heat until shimmering (about 350°F). Line one baking sheet with paper towels, and have an unlined baking sheet ready.

7. Wrap tortillas in damp paper towels, and microwave until warm and pliable, 30 seconds. Lay 1 tortilla on a flat surface, and add a heaping ¼ cup of shredded beef onto bottom third of tortilla. Tightly roll up, and place seam side down on the unlined baking sheet. (If desired, use a wooden toothpick to secure; just be sure to remove before eating.) Repeat with remaining tortillas and beef. (You may have some beef left over.)

8. Add 4 flautas to hot oil, seam sides down. Fry, turning occasionally, until golden brown all over, 3 to 4 minutes. Transfer to paper towel–lined baking sheet. Repeat with remaining flautas. Serve immediately with desired toppings and lime wedges.

Pomegranate Guacamole

California's Pinnacles National Park offers more than 30 miles of hiking trails through scenic valleys, across grassy meadows, and past its iconic rock formations. There are also unique talus caves, which are created by boulders falling into narrow canyons. When you're done exploring, head to one of the nearby towns for a cool drink and a snack. Chips and guacamole is always a good call, and pomegranates, which are grown not too far from the park, make the perfect crunchy addition to the classic dip.

YIELD: 4 SERVINGS
HANDS-ON TIME: 15 MINUTES
TOTAL TIME: 15 MINUTES

3 ripe Haas avocados, peeled and pitted

2 or 3 limes, halved

1 large clove garlic, grated

¾ teaspoon kosher salt, plus more for seasoning

⅓ cup fresh cilantro leaves and tender stems, finely chopped

½ cup pomegranate arils, divided

1. In a large bowl, mash together avocados, juice from 2 limes, garlic, and salt to desired texture using a potato masher or fork. Use a spoon or silicone spatula to mix in cilantro and all but 1 tablespoon of the pomegranate arils. Season to taste with more lime juice and salt.

2. Transfer guacamole to a serving bowl. Top with remaining pomegranate arils, and serve.

Recipe Note

If not serving immediately, cover with plastic wrap, pressing it directly against the surface of the guacamole, and refrigerate. Do not make more than a few hours ahead, or the guacamole will begin to brown.

Dungeness Crab Cakes

Nearly 40 miles of untamed coastline are protected in Redwood National and State Parks in Northern California. This means that besides viewing the massive, jaw-dropping trees, visitors can also meander the Pacific Ocean's edge, marvel at cliffs, and perhaps even spot a gray whale. Of course, the sea's bounty also provides a delicious meal at the end of a drive or a hike. At Moonstone Bar & Grill in Trinidad, California, diners can feast on these Dungeness crab cakes, if the West Coast crustacean is in season (usually November through July).

YIELD: 4 SERVINGS
HANDS-ON TIME: 30 MINUTES
TOTAL TIME: 1 HOUR 5 MINUTES, INCLUDING CHILLING

1 pound Dungeness or regular lump crab meat

1 cup panko breadcrumbs, toasted and cooled

1 cup mayonnaise

1 tablespoon chopped fresh parsley, plus more for serving

1 tablespoon chopped fresh dill, plus more for serving

1 tablespoon sriracha hot sauce

1 lemon, halved

3 tablespoons vegetable oil

1. In a large bowl, gently mix crab meat, panko, mayonnaise, parsley, dill, sriracha, and juice from 1 lemon half until well combined. Form into 8 (2½-inch-round) patties. Place on a plate or small baking sheet and chill until firm, about 30 minutes.

2. Cut remaining lemon half into wedges. In a large nonstick skillet, heat oil over medium-high heat, adjusting heat as necessary to avoid burning. Add crab cakes, and cook until browned, 4 to 5 minutes per side. Serve crab cakes with lemon wedges and more parsley and dill.

A hiker explores the Leiffer Loop Trail.

Wild Mushroom Pasta

Near the top of California lie Redwood National and State Parks, renowned for the world's tallest trees. While the ancient, towering marvels might be the first thing to catch your eye, the dense forests are also filled with native plants, many of which are edible. Redwood's laws allow the foraging of all berries for personal consumption (huckleberries, salmonberries, thimbleberries, and blackberries are found throughout the woods). On the other hand, gathering any of the 200-some species of mushrooms—which proliferate in Redwood—is not permitted. Luckily, a wide variety of mushrooms are readily available for purchase nowadays, so pick up some of your favorites and create a forest-inspired feast at home.

YIELD: 4 SERVINGS
HANDS-ON TIME: 40 MINUTES
TOTAL TIME: 40 MINUTES

Kosher salt

1 pound campanelle, penne, or other short-noodle pasta

3 tablespoons unsalted butter, divided

2 tablespoons olive oil, divided

1 pound mixed wild mushrooms (such as hen of the woods, oyster, and chanterelle), chopped or torn into bite-size pieces

1 large shallot, halved and thinly sliced

4 large cloves garlic, thinly sliced

½ cup walnuts, toasted and chopped (optional)

Pepper

½ cup dry white wine, mushroom stock, or water

½ cup heavy cream

⅓ cup grated Parmesan cheese, plus more for serving

½ lemon

Minced fresh chives (optional)

1. Bring a large pot of salted water to a boil. Add pasta and cook according to package directions until al dente. Reserve 1 cup pasta cooking water, then drain pasta.

2. While pasta cooks, melt 2 tablespoons butter with 1 tablespoon oil in a large skillet over medium-high heat. Stir in mushrooms. Cook, stirring occasionally, until mushrooms start to brown, 8 to 10 minutes.

3. Reduce heat to medium. Add remaining 1 tablespoon oil. Stir in shallot and garlic. Cook, stirring occasionally, until shallot is softened, 2 to 3 minutes. Stir in walnuts, if using, then season with salt and pepper.

4. Pour wine into pan. Cook, stirring constantly, until liquid is mostly absorbed, about 2 minutes. Stir in cooked pasta, heavy cream, and ⅔ cup reserved pasta water. Bring to a simmer, and cook, stirring constantly, until sauce has slightly thickened, about 1 minute.

5. Remove from heat. Add Parmesan, remaining 1 tablespoon butter, and a squeeze of lemon juice; stir, adding more pasta water, a couple tablespoons at a time, if needed, until sauce is glossy and coats the pasta. Season with salt, pepper, and lemon juice, if desired.

6. Serve pasta immediately with more Parmesan and chives, if desired.

Lamb T-Bones With Garlic, Ginger & Honey Sauce

Estes Park, Colorado, is often a home base for visitors to Rocky Mountain National Park. Because of this, the town earned the nickname the Gateway to the Rockies, and its downtown area is packed with not only places to stay but also great spots to eat after spending the day bouldering, biking, or hiking. Bird & Jim—named after Isabella Bird, a Scottish traveler "seized" by the Rockies, and outdoor guide "Mountain Jim"—celebrates Colorado cuisine by using as many local ingredients as possible, including beef, lamb, and game meats.

YIELD: 4 SERVINGS
HANDS-ON TIME: 45 MINUTES
TOTAL TIME: 45 MINUTES

8 (5- to 6-ounce, 1-inch-thick) lamb loin chops (also known as lamb T-bone steaks)

½ cup honey

1 (2-inch) piece ginger, peeled and finely minced

3 tablespoons soy sauce

2 tablespoons minced shallot

2 tablespoons minced garlic

1 tablespoon Worcestershire sauce

2 teaspoons Dijon mustard

¼ teaspoon Aleppo chile flakes or crushed red pepper, plus more for seasoning

1 lime, zested and halved

3 tablespoons chopped fresh cilantro, plus more for serving

Kosher salt

Pepper

1 tablespoon vegetable oil

Microgreens (optional)

1. Pat loin chops dry with paper towels. Let stand at room temperature while preparing the sauce.

2. In a small pot, combine honey, ginger, soy sauce, shallot, garlic, Worcestershire, Dijon, and chile flakes. Bring to a simmer over medium heat. Reduce heat to low, and cook, stirring frequently, until reduced and thickened, 10 to 13 minutes.

3. Remove from heat. Stir in lime zest and juice from half of lime. Transfer to a blender, and process until smooth. Return sauce to pot, and stir in cilantro. Season with more salt, lime juice, and chile flakes, if desired. Cover and keep warm over low heat, if needed.

4. Season chops on both sides with salt and pepper. Heat a large cast-iron or stainless-steel skillet over medium-high heat. Add chops, and cook until browned on both sides and cooked to desired doneness, turning once, 3 to 4 minutes per side for medium-rare.

5. Serve chops with sauce, microgreens (if desired), and more cilantro.

Ensalada de Nopales

Named after the nation's largest cactus, Saguaro National Park is situated in the Sonoran Desert in southern Arizona. Saguaro cactuses can grow as tall as 50 feet, but that height takes time—in the first 10 years of its life, the cactus creeps up only a few inches. Flowers don't start to appear until the succulent reaches 35 years old, but they continue to bloom throughout its lifespan, which can be as long as 200 years. Arizona law protects the saguaro—a symbol of the American Southwest and a sacred plant for some Native Americans—and the park prohibits foraging of any kind. Outside the park, the fruit and paddles of other cactuses, like the prickly pear cactus in this salad, are fair game for medicinal purposes and human consumption.

YIELD: 4 SERVINGS

HANDS-ON TIME: 35 MINUTES

TOTAL TIME: 2 HOURS 45 MINUTES, INCLUDING CHILLING

1 pound nopales (cactus paddles)

2 tablespoons olive or vegetable oil, divided

1½ teaspoons kosher salt, divided

1 to 2 limes

1 small white onion, diced

1 beefsteak or 3 Roma tomatoes, diced

1 small jalapeño pepper, thinly sliced (seeded, if desired)

¼ cup fresh cilantro leaves and tender stems, chopped, plus more for serving

1 tablespoon fresh oregano leaves, chopped, or 1 teaspoon dried (preferably Mexican)

1 radish, thinly sliced

Queso fresco, crumbled

1. Carefully wash nopales, then pat dry with paper towels; lay flat on a cutting board. Trim ¼ inch from edge of each nopal. Using a paring knife, remove thorns and bumps, keeping as much skin intact as possible. Slice into 1-inch squares.

2. Heat 1 tablespoon oil in a large nonstick skillet over medium-high heat. Stir in nopales and 1 teaspoon salt. Cook, without stirring, until nopales begin to brown, about 2 minutes; stir and cook 2 minutes more. Reduce heat to medium-low, and cover skillet; cook, stirring occasionally, until softened and browned in spots, about 15 minutes. If there is still gelatinous liquid in the skillet, stir, cover, and cook until liquid has evaporated, up to 3 minutes more.

3. Transfer nopales to a serving bowl and cool for 10 minutes. Zest 1 lime, and halve both; add zest and juice from 1 lime to nopales. Stir in onion, tomato, jalapeño, cilantro, oregano, and remaining 1 tablespoon oil and ½ teaspoon salt. Season with more salt and lime juice, if needed.

4. Cover with plastic wrap, and refrigerate for 2 hours or up to overnight. Stir before topping with radish, queso fresco, and cilantro.

Recipe Note

Football-shaped bolillo rolls have a crispy crust and soft interior and are traditional for Sonoran hot dogs. If they're hard to find, substitute a French baguette cut into four 6-inch-long pieces.

Sonoran Hot Dogs

Although Sonoran-style hot dogs originated in Mexico, the regional specialty made its way across the U.S. border and became popular—so much so that you can find them on menus around Tucson, Arizona, just outside Saguaro National Park. Traditionally, Sonoran hot dogs are wrapped in bacon and nestled in a pillowy bolillo roll with smashed pinto beans and a load of toppings. The dish makes for a quick, filling meal in between sightseeing, and it's fairly simple to re-create the experience at home—minus views of the majestic saguaro cactuses.

YIELD: 4 SERVINGS

HANDS-ON TIME: 40 MINUTES

TOTAL TIME: 40 MINUTES

1 tablespoon olive or vegetable oil

1 medium white onion, diced

1 (15.5-ounce) can pinto beans, drained and rinsed

1 teaspoon garlic powder

½ teaspoon ground cumin

½ cup water

Kosher salt

4 hot dogs

8 thin slices bacon

4 bolillo rolls, split two-thirds of the way through (see note)

For serving: sliced avocado, diced tomatoes, sliced jalapeño peppers, crumbled queso fresco, crema or sour cream, yellow mustard

1. Heat oil in a large skillet over medium heat. Stir in onion, and cook until it starts to soften, about 3 minutes. Add beans, garlic powder, and cumin. Cook, stirring constantly, for 2 minutes. Add ½ cup water, bring to a simmer, and cook for 5 minutes, adding more water by the table-spoonful if mixture becomes too dry. Smash beans with a fork a few times, then cook until thickened, 2 to 3 minutes. Season with salt, if needed. Remove from heat, and cover to keep warm.

2. Preheat grill or a large grill pan over medium heat (300°F to 350°F). Tightly wrap each hot dog with 2 slices of bacon, tuck-ing in ends of bacon to secure. Grill hot dogs, covered with grill lid and turning a few times, until bacon is crisp and hot dogs are heated through, 8 to 10 minutes.

3. Spread a few tablespoons of bean mixture on bottom of each roll. Add hot dogs and desired toppings. Serve immediately.

Towering saguaro cactuses

Sequioa National Park

Standing more than 250 feet tall, Sentinel Tree is one of the largest sequoias in the Giant Forest and has been welcoming visitors to the Giant Forest Museum for years.

Trout Almondine With Rice Pilaf

The ancient, towering sequoias—some of the world's largest trees, by volume—shade the namesake national park's forest and grow at a high elevation in the Sierra Nevada mountains, providing a cool climate for the wildlife underneath the canopy. A number of rivers run through this California national park, and their chilly waters are the perfect temperature for several species of native trout to thrive. If fishing isn't on your activity list, make a reservation at The Peaks Restaurant in Wuksachi Lodge, nestled in the heart of the park, and order the trout almondine for a taste of the freshwater fish.

YIELD: 4 SERVINGS
HANDS-ON TIME: 30 MINUTES
TOTAL TIME: 30 MINUTES

RICE PILAF

1 tablespoon olive oil or butter

¼ cup finely chopped onion

¼ cup finely chopped celery

1 cup uncooked long-grain white rice

1¾ cups chicken or vegetable stock

Kosher salt and pepper

TROUT

4 (5- to 7-ounce) skin-on trout fillets

Kosher salt and pepper

⅓ cup all-purpose flour

¼ cup (½ stick) unsalted butter, divided

¼ cup sliced almonds

¼ cup slivered almonds

1 lemon, halved

2 tablespoons chopped fresh parsley

1. To make the pilaf, in a medium saucepan, heat oil over medium heat. Add onion and celery. Cook, stirring occasionally, until softened, 3 to 4 minutes. Add rice, and cook, stirring frequently, until grains become slightly translucent, 1 to 2 minutes.

2. Pour in stock. Bring to a boil, then reduce heat to low. Cover, and simmer until rice is tender and liquid is absorbed, about 15 minutes. Remove from heat, and let stand, covered, for 5 minutes. Fluff with a fork, and season with salt and pepper. Cover to keep warm.

3. While rice cooks, make the trout. Pat trout dry with paper towels. Season both sides with salt and pepper. Place flour on a plate or bowl, and coat fish in flour, shaking off any excess.

4. In a large skillet, melt 1 tablespoon butter over medium-high heat. Cook 2 trout fillets in skillet until golden brown and cooked through, 2 to 3 minutes per side. Transfer to a clean plate, and loosely tent with foil to keep warm. Repeat with 1 tablespoon butter and remaining trout fillets.

5. Wipe skillet clean, then return to burner over medium heat. Melt remaining 2 tablespoons butter in skillet, then add sliced almonds and slivered almonds. Cook, stirring frequently, until golden brown and fragrant, 2 to 3 minutes, being mindful of burning. Remove from heat, stir in juice from half of lemon and parsley. Season sauce with salt and pepper.

6. Cut remaining lemon half into wedges. Serve trout with pilaf, sauce, and lemon wedges.

Mile-High Blackberry Ice Cream Pie

At the highest point on Shenandoah National Park's iconic Skyline Drive, you'll find Skyland, the historic Virginia resort that opened in the late 1800s. Skyland's Pollock Dining Room has striking views of the Shenandoah Valley and a menu inspired by the region. No matter what you order for your entrée, you can't miss a slice of the Mile-High Blackberry Ice Cream Pie for dessert. The towering treat—with its berry ice cream, berry sauce, and fluffy cap of toasted meringue—was inspired by the blackberry thickets that pop up all over the Blue Ridge Mountains each summer.

YIELD: 8 SERVINGS

HANDS-ON TIME: 45 MINUTES

TOTAL TIME: 13 HOURS, INCLUDING COOLING AND FREEZING

1 store-bought graham cracker piecrust

½ gallon (64 ounces) blackberry ice cream, slightly softened

4 large egg whites at room temperature

2 cups granulated sugar, divided

½ teaspoon kosher salt

½ teaspoon vanilla extract

1 large orange

1 lemon

2 cups fresh blackberries, plus more for garnish

2 tablespoons cornstarch

1. Preheat oven to 375°F. Bake piecrust until crisp and slightly darkened, about 6 minutes. Let crust cool completely, about 10 to 15 minutes.

2. Scoop ice cream into cooled crust, spreading evenly and mounding in center. Freeze until ice cream is very hard, at least 3 hours.

3. In the bowl of a stand mixer fitted with a whisk attachment (or using a handheld mixer), beat egg whites until frothy, about 1 minute. With mixer running, slowly pour in ½ cup sugar, salt, and vanilla. Beat until mixture is glossy and soft peaks form, 2 to 3 minutes. Spread over ice cream, swirling into decorative peaks with the back of a large spoon. Return pie to freezer, and freeze at least 8 hours.

4. Squeeze juice from orange to equal ¼ cup and from lemon to equal 2 tablespoons. In a medium saucepan, cook juices, blackberries, and remaining 1½ cups sugar over medium-low heat, whisking often, until berries break down and mixture reaches a syrup consistency, 6 to 8 minutes. Gradually whisk in cornstarch, and cook until sauce thickens, about 2 minutes.

5. Preheat broiler, and place pie on a baking sheet. Broil until meringue is browned, about 5 minutes. (If you have a kitchen torch, you can save time and use it here.) Serve pie with sauce and additional berries.

Hiking in Shenandoah

Country Ham With Red-Eye Gravy & Grits

In the Shenandoah Valley, country ham is king. In the early 1600s, English colonists brought their pigs to Virginia and combined European and Native American techniques to create the salt-cured pork. Centuries later, the production of country ham continues, and some attribute the success to the climate of the valley: It's part of the "Ham Belt," a strip of climate zone around the world ideal for preserving meat. The Blue Ridge Mountains, which run right through Shenandoah National Park, help shape the weather of this ham-curing region.

YIELD: 2 TO 3 SERVINGS
HANDS-ON TIME: 30 MINUTES
TOTAL TIME: 30 MINUTES

2 cups water

Kosher salt

½ cup old-fashioned grits

5 tablespoons unsalted butter, divided

Freshly cracked black pepper

2 or 3 (¼-inch-thick) country ham slices (about 12 ounces)

⅔ cup freshly brewed coffee

1 teaspoon brown sugar

1. In a small pot, bring 2 cups water and a large pinch of salt to a boil. Once boiling, slowly whisk in grits. Reduce heat to medium-low, cover, and simmer until water is absorbed and grits are tender, about 15 minutes. Remove from heat, and stir in 3 tablespoons butter; season with salt and pepper to taste.

2. Meanwhile, melt 1 tablespoon butter in a large skillet over medium heat. Add ham in an even layer (working in batches if necessary), and cook until browned, 3 minutes per side. Transfer to a plate.

3. Pour coffee and brown sugar into skillet. Bring to a simmer, scraping bottom of skillet to release any browned bits. Simmer until slightly reduced, about 2 minutes. (The gravy won't be thick; it will look more like a jus.) Remove from heat, and add remaining 1 tablespoon butter.

4. Serve ham immediately over grits with gravy, sprinkled generously with pepper.

Bison Osso Buco

Theodore Roosevelt's relationship with bison ended differently than it began. In 1883, he came to the Dakota Territory to hunt the game animal. The task proved difficult, as the herds were being depleted by commercial hunters. He moved on to cattle ranching, but eventually lost ranches to overgrazing. Through all this, Roosevelt began to see the negative effects humans could have on natural resources and made it his mission to protect America's land and wildlife. This osso buco, made with local farm-raised bison, is a nod to the conservationist and one of the most popular dishes at Theodore's Dining Room in Medora, North Dakota, just outside the park.

YIELD: 4 SERVINGS
HANDS-ON TIME: 45 MINUTES
TOTAL TIME: 2 HOURS 25 MINUTES

4 bison or veal shanks
(3½ to 4 pounds)

1 tablespoon paprika

Kosher salt

1 tablespoon rice flour

Theodore Roosevelt

3 tablespoons vegetable oil, divided

2 large carrots, cut into ½-inch pieces

1 large onion, chopped

1 stalk celery, chopped

6 cloves garlic, chopped

1 small bunch fresh thyme

3 fresh rosemary sprigs

2 bay leaves

2 tablespoons tomato paste

1¼ cups dry red wine

1 cup veal demi-glace, diluted, if necessary, according to package directions

1 teaspoon beef bouillon base (such as Better Than Bouillon)

Pepper

Mashed potatoes, for serving (optional)

1. Preheat oven to 325°F. Pat bison dry with paper towels. Season all over with paprika and salt, then sprinkle with rice flour.

2. Heat 2 tablespoons oil in a large Dutch oven or heavy-bottomed pot over medium-high heat. Cook bison, in batches, turning once, until browned, 2 to 3 minutes per side. Transfer to a plate.

3. Add remaining 1 tablespoon oil to Dutch oven. Stir in carrots, onion, and celery. Cook, stirring occasionally, until vegetables start to soften, 3 to 5 minutes. Add garlic, thyme, rosemary, and bay leaves; cook, stirring constantly, for 2 minutes. Stir in tomato paste, and cook for 1 minute.

4. Pour in wine. Bring to a boil, scraping bottom of Dutch oven to release any browned bits. Stir in demi-glace and beef base. Bring to a boil, then reduce heat to a simmer. Return bison to Dutch oven. (The braising liquid should come three-quarters of the way up the bison; if it doesn't, add water until it reaches this point.)

5. Cover Dutch oven and transfer to oven. Slow-roast until bison is fork-tender and liquid has reduced, 1½ to 2 hours. Season braising liquid with salt and pepper. Serve osso buco over mashed potatoes, if desired.

Fat Rascals

A book about the U.S. national parks would not be complete without mentioning Theodore Roosevelt, who is known as the "conservationist president." During his administration, he helped protect an estimated 230 million acres of land; established 23 sites for the park system; and created federal bird reservations and game preserves, forerunners to today's national wildlife refuges. To honor his legacy, a park was named after him in North Dakota. Besides the outdoors, Roosevelt loved a good meal. He was particularly fond of his wife Edith's "fat rascals": poppable currant-studded biscuits that she would make for breakfast and snacking.

YIELD: 1 DOZEN BISCUITS

HANDS-ON TIME: 25 MINUTES

TOTAL TIME: 50 MINUTES, INCLUDING SOAKING

---

1 cup dried currants or raisins

2 cups (240 grams) all-purpose flour

¼ cup (50 grams) granulated sugar, divided

2 teaspoons baking powder

½ teaspoon kosher salt

¾ cup (1½ sticks) unsalted butter, cut into cubes and chilled

⅔ cup (160 milliliters) heavy cream, half-and-half, or whole milk, plus more for brushing

1. Place currants in a small bowl and cover with hot water. Let soak for 10 minutes, then pour through a fine-mesh strainer to drain. Rinse quickly with cold water to cool, and drain well again.

2. Preheat oven to 450°F. Line a baking sheet with parchment paper.

3. In a large bowl, whisk together flour, 3 tablespoons sugar, baking powder, and salt until combined. Add butter. Combine mixture using your hands, breaking butter into pea-size pieces. Mix in drained currants until evenly distributed.

4. Make a well in center of mixture. Slowly pour in cream, and use a fork to incorporate into flour mixture to make a shaggy dough. Use your hands to gather and gently press dough together, incorporating any remaining flour. (Do not overwork.)

5. Transfer dough to a clean surface, then roll to 1-inch thickness. Use a 2-inch biscuit cutter to cut into rounds. Transfer rounds to prepared baking sheet, evenly spaced apart. Gently reroll dough scraps, and cut out more rounds. Brush tops of rounds with cream, and sprinkle with remaining 1 tablespoon sugar.

6. Bake until golden brown, 12 to 14 minutes. Transfer to a wire rack to cool slightly; serve warm.

Little Missouri River

*Blackened Mahi-Mahi
With Mango-Rum Sauce
(page 218) and Fried
Plantains (page 219)*

Blackened Mahi-Mahi With Mango-Rum Sauce

Virgin Islands National Park protects two-thirds of St. John, a 28-square-mile island in the Caribbean. The small but mighty island has a lot going on: a 3,000-year-old history of the first settlers, the Taino people; rocky and lush terrain with loads of trails; and rich coral reefs and deep ocean waters that make it a prime spot for snorkeling, scuba diving, and fishing. Sharks, dolphins, sea turtles, stingrays, and the occasional whale can all be spotted swimming around the island. There's also spiny lobster, conch, and a wide array of fish, including barracuda, grouper, and mahi-mahi. Seafood restaurant Morgan's Mango, outside the park, serves up this fresh catch with its signature mango-rum sauce—two ingredients that also have local ties.

YIELD: 4 SERVINGS
HANDS-ON TIME: 30 MINUTES
TOTAL TIME: 30 MINUTES

1 large ripe mango, peeled and pitted (or 12 ounces frozen, thawed mango)

2 tablespoons butter, divided

3 tablespoons dark rum

1 tablespoon sour cream

1 lime, zested and quartered, plus more for serving

Kosher salt

4 (6- to 8-ounce) skin-on mahi-mahi fillets

1 tablespoon blackening or Cajun seasoning

1 tablespoon vegetable oil

Microgreens and warm cooked rice (optional)

1. Add mango to a blender, and process until smooth. Melt 1 tablespoon butter in a medium saucepan over medium heat. Stir in mango and rum. Bring to a simmer, and cook, stirring occasionally, for 5 minutes. Remove from heat, and stir in sour cream and lime zest. Season with lime juice and salt. Cover and keep warm.

2. Pat fish dry with paper towels. Sprinkle both sides of fish with salt, then rub with blackening seasoning.

3. Melt remaining 1 tablespoon butter with oil in a large nonstick pan over medium-high heat. Add fish, skin sides down, and fry until skin is browned and crisp, about 4 minutes. Flip fish, and fry until fully cooked, about 3 minutes.

4. Transfer fish to plates, and spoon mango-rum sauce on top; serve with lime wedges. If desired, top with microgreens and serve with rice.

Fried Plantains

Like many spots in the Caribbean, the U.S. Virgin Islands has a challenging past. In the early 1600s, European slave ships transported millions of African people to the islands to a life of bondage. Water and food were scarce, especially on St. John, now home to Virgin Islands National Park. The enslavers brought inexpensive and filling bananas and plantains on ships to feed the enslaved men and women. Eventually, the crops became plentiful and versatile on the islands and are now considered staples in the Caribbean. Morgan's Mango, a favorite seafood spot on St. John, lets the sweet, starchy fruit shine with a quick fry and a little salt.

YIELD: 4 SERVINGS
HANDS-ON TIME: 20 MINUTES
TOTAL TIME: 20 MINUTES

3 large ripe plantains

Vegetable oil, for frying

Kosher salt

1. Line a baking sheet with paper towels. Peel plantains, and slice on an angle into ½-inch-thick pieces.

2. Pour ½ inch oil into a medium skillet, and heat over medium heat. Fry plantains, in batches, 2 minutes per side, then transfer with a slotted spoon to prepared baking sheet, and sprinkle with salt. Serve immediately.

Fried Walleye Fingers With Simple Tartar Sauce

With 30 lakes within Voyageurs National Park, it would be a shame to visit and not go fishing. Novice and experienced anglers need to get only a Minnesota fishing license to try their hand at snagging any of the 54 fish species in the park. For a true Minnesota experience, catch some walleye and fry them up for what's known as a "shore lunch," an outdoor fish fry that's done right on the lakeshore. In this recipe, the breading is super simple—just eggs, flour, and crushed saltines that you smash right in the (unopened) sleeve. It's simple food at its best.

YIELD: 6 APPETIZER SERVINGS
HANDS-ON TIME: 30 MINUTES
TOTAL TIME: 30 MINUTES

SIMPLE TARTAR SAUCE

½ cup mayonnaise

3 tablespoons finely chopped dill pickles, plus 2 teaspoons pickle juice

1 tablespoon lemon juice

Pepper

FRIED WALLEYE FINGERS

Vegetable oil, for frying

1 pound walleye, cod, or other whitefish fillets, cut into 1-inch-thick planks

½ cup all-purpose flour

½ teaspoon kosher salt, plus more for seasoning

½ teaspoon pepper, plus more for seasoning

2 large eggs, beaten

1 sleeve saltine crackers, finely crushed (about 1¼ cups)

Lemon wedges

1. To make the tartar sauce, in a small bowl, stir together mayonnaise, chopped pickles, pickle juice, and lemon juice. Season with pepper.

2. To make the fish, pour 2 inches oil into a large pot or Dutch oven, and heat over medium heat until it reaches 350°F, about 10 minutes.

3. Meanwhile, season fish on all sides with salt and pepper. In a shallow bowl, stir together flour, ½ teaspoon salt, and ½ teaspoon pepper. In another shallow bowl, beat eggs. Put crushed saltine crackers in a third shallow bowl.

4. Coat fish, one piece at a time, in flour mixture and then in egg mixture, letting excess drip off. Coat in saltines, pressing so the fish is thoroughly covered. Transfer to a baking sheet or large plate.

5. Arrange a wire rack in a baking sheet. Fry fish, in batches and turning once, until it is golden and cooked through and flakes easily with a fork, 2 to 3 minutes. Transfer to wire rack, and sprinkle with salt while hot. Serve with tartar sauce and lemon wedges.

Recipe Note

Walleye skin is very thin, so you can leave it on for this recipe. If you're using whitefish, it's best to remove the skin (your grocer's fishmonger can do it for you).

Christmas Chiles Rellenos

Its 275 square miles of gypsum sand dunefields give White Sands its name and unique, otherworldly appearance. Visitors can hike through the dunes or sled down their slopes in designated areas. There are no restaurants in this land of sparkling sand, but there are lots of great options nearby, including many outstanding Mexican spots. These chiles rellenos are inspired by the classic Mexican dish, which is also especially popular in New Mexico, where the park is located. Serving the stuffed and fried peppers "Christmas style" is the New Mexican way of ordering a dish with both green and red chile sauce. The leftover sauces are great on eggs, tacos, and burritos and with chicken, steak, pork, and lamb.

YIELD: 6 SERVINGS
HANDS-ON TIME: 1 HOUR
TOTAL TIME: 1 HOUR 10 MINUTES

HATCH GREEN CHILE SAUCE

2 tablespoons olive or vegetable oil

1 cup chopped white or yellow onion

½ teaspoon salt

3 cloves garlic, finely chopped

¼ teaspoon ground cumin

¼ teaspoon dried oregano

1 tablespoon all-purpose flour

1 cup (8 ounces) roasted and chopped Hatch chiles

1½ cups chicken or pork stock

RED CHILE SAUCE

2 ounces dried New Mexico, Anaheim, or Guajillo chiles (about 5 to 7 chiles)

1 tablespoon olive or vegetable oil

1 cup chopped white or yellow onion

1 large clove garlic, finely chopped

2 cups chicken or pork stock

1 teaspoon honey

½ teaspoon salt

¼ teaspoon ground cumin

¼ teaspoon dried oregano

CHILES RELLENOS

6 large poblano chiles

Vegetable oil, for frying

8 ounces Asadero, Oaxacan, or Monterey Jack cheese, cut into 6 (4-by-½-inch) sticks

3 large eggs, separated

½ cup all-purpose flour

½ teaspoon kosher salt, plus more for seasoning

Cotija cheese (optional)

1. To make the green chile sauce, in a large skillet, heat oil over medium heat. Add onion, sprinkle with salt, and cook until softened, 3 to 4 minutes. Add garlic, and cook until fragrant, about 1 minute. Add cumin and oregano, and cook 1 minute. Sprinkle flour over onion mixture, and cook, stirring constantly, until flour is very light tan, about 2 minutes. Stir in chiles, then slowly stir in stock. Bring to a boil, reduce heat, and simmer until thickened, about 15 minutes. Season with salt to taste. If desired, puree half or all of sauce in a blender to desired consistency.

2. To make the red chile sauce, stem and seed chiles (use gloves if you have sensitive skin). In a large skillet, heat oil over medium heat. Add chiles and toast, turning occasionally, until fragrant, about 3 minutes. Transfer to a plate. Add onion and garlic to skillet, adding more oil if needed. Cook, stirring frequently, until onions soften, about 5 minutes. Add stock and return chiles to skillet. Simmer until chiles soften, about 5 minutes.

3. Carefully transfer mixture to a blender. Holding the top with a potholder, blend until mostly smooth. Pour through a fine-mesh strainer into skillet; discard solids. Stir in honey, salt, cumin, and oregano. Bring to a simmer over medium-low heat, and let cook until heated through, about 5 minutes.

4. To make the chiles rellenos, roast chiles over a gas flame or in the broiler, turning occasionally, until skins are mostly blackened.

(Continued on page 224)

(Continued from page 222)

5. Transfer to a bowl, cover with plastic wrap, and let steam. Once chiles are cool enough to handle, peel off skins (it's okay if there's a bit of skin left).

6. Pour 2 inches oil into a large pot or deep skillet; heat over medium-high to 350°F. Arrange a wire rack in a large baking sheet.

7. Cut a small slit in top of each chile. Carefully insert one cheese stick inside each.

8. In a medium bowl, using an electric mixer, beat egg whites until stiff peaks form. With the mixer on low, add egg yolks, one at a time, beating until blended after each addition. The batter should be pale yellow and very fluffy.

9. Stir together flour and salt in a shallow bowl. Coat one chile in flour, gently shaking to remove excess. Dip in eggs, coating completely. Fry in hot oil until golden, 3 to 5 minutes per side. Transfer to wire rack, and sprinkle with salt while hot. Repeat with remaining chiles.

10. Serve chiles with both sauces. Garnish with cotija, if desired.

Pistachio Brittle

Part of the thrill of visiting national parks is getting a glimpse into a very specific part of the country. White Sands is known for its sparkling sand dunes, but while you're visiting the area, be sure to build in a little time to explore outside the park. One specific local gem is PistachioLand in Alamogordo, New Mexico, about a 25-minute drive from White Sands. To find the spot, look for the World's Largest Pistachio, and get ready to stock up on the nut and pistachio-based treats. Don't miss grabbing some pistachio brittle for snacking on pre– or post–sand sliding in the park—or make this version at home.

YIELD: 24 SERVINGS
HANDS-ON TIME: 30 MINUTES
TOTAL TIME: 30 MINUTES,
NOT INCLUDING COOLING

2 cups granulated sugar

1 cup water

⅔ cup light corn syrup

¾ teaspoon kosher salt

3 cups roasted and salted shelled pistachios

¼ cup (½ stick) butter, cubed

2 teaspoons vanilla extract

¾ teaspoon baking soda

1. Line an 18-by-13-inch baking sheet with parchment paper.

2. In a medium Dutch oven or heavy-bottomed pot fitted with a candy thermometer, combine sugar with 1 cup water, corn syrup, and salt over medium heat. (Make sure the candy thermometer is in the syrup and not touching the bottom of the pot.) Cook, stirring occasionally, until it comes to a gentle boil. (The timing on this will vary—it can take anywhere from a few minutes to more than 15; it takes patience!)

3. Continue boiling, stirring occasionally, until temperature registers 280°F. Stir in pistachios, butter, vanilla, and baking soda. (The mixture will foam after the baking soda is added.) Return to a gentle boil, and cook, stirring often, until temperature reaches 300°F.

4. Working quickly, pour mixture onto prepared baking sheet, and use a silicone spatula to spread it into an even layer, as close to the edges of the pan as possible. Cool completely at room temperature.

5. Break apart using a mallet or your hands. Store in an airtight container at room temperature for up to a month.

225

Buffalo Chislic

South Dakota's Wind Cave National Park is best known for the upwards of 450 bison roaming its grasslands and for Wind Cave, a long, complex cave system and a place of deep significance among different Indigenous peoples, especially the Lakota. After exploring the world above- and belowground at the park, it's time for another South Dakota original: chislic, a classic dish that consists of deep-fried cubes of meat served with saltines and a sauce (often ranch dressing).

YIELD: 6 APPETIZER SERVINGS
HANDS-ON TIME: 30 MINUTES
TOTAL TIME: 3 HOURS, INCLUDING MARINATING AND STANDING

1½ pounds bison, beef, venison, or lamb sirloin roast, trimmed and cut into 1-inch cubes

2 tablespoons Worcestershire sauce

1 teaspoon garlic powder

1 teaspoon kosher salt

Vegetable oil, for frying

Ranch dressing and saltine crackers, for serving

1. Toss together bison, Worcestershire, garlic powder, and salt in a medium bowl. Marinate in refrigerator for 2 to 3 hours.

2. Remove bison from refrigerator, and let stand 30 minutes at room temperature.

3. Pour 2 inches oil into a large, heavy-bottomed pot, and heat to 350°F. Arrange a wire rack in a baking sheet. Fry bison, in batches, until browned and cooked to desired doneness, about 1 to 2 minutes. Using a slotted spoon, transfer to prepared baking sheet to drain. Serve chislic with ranch and saltines.

The park's first visitors center

Copper River Salmon Roll

Covering more than 13 million acres, Wrangell-St. Elias is the largest of the U.S. national parks (a whopping six Yellowstones could fit inside). The rugged landscape begins at the ocean, near the Gulf of Alaska, and climbs to 18,008 feet on the top of Mount St. Elias, the second highest peak in the United States. There are other grand mountains within the park, as well as massive glaciers, volcanoes, conifer-rich forests, and a giant network of rivers and streams. The Copper River is perhaps the most famous of the waterways, known for the two million–plus salmon that swim up the glacially fed streams to spawn. The Potato, a roadside restaurant inside Wrangell-St. Elias, highlights this incredible fish, loading it on a buttery roll.

YIELD: 6 ROLLS
HANDS-ON TIME: 20 MINUTES
TOTAL TIME: 1 HOUR 30 MINUTES, INCLUDING COOLING AND CHILLING

SALMON SALAD

1½ pounds sockeye salmon fillets

1½ teaspoons kosher salt, divided

1 tablespoon extra-virgin olive oil

1 small red bell pepper, seeded and finely diced

4 green onions, trimmed and thinly sliced

¼ cup mayonnaise

3 tablespoons fresh lemon juice

1 teaspoon dried tarragon, or 1 tablespoon chopped fresh

½ teaspoon white or black pepper

¼ teaspoon ground mustard

Pinch of cayenne pepper

VINAIGRETTE

½ cup fresh lemon juice

½ cup neutral oil, such as grapeseed or vegetable

¼ cup extra-virgin olive oil

1 tablespoon Dijon mustard

2 teaspoons granulated sugar

1 teaspoon kosher salt

ROLLS

6 hoagie rolls

2 tablespoons butter, melted

1 romaine heart, thinly sliced

2 medium tomatoes, finely diced

1. To make the salmon salad, preheat oven to 375°F. Line a baking sheet with aluminum foil. Pat salmon dry with paper towels, then place on prepared baking sheet. Season with 1 teaspoon salt, and drizzle with oil.

2. Bake until cooked through, 14 to 18 minutes. Cool slightly, then cover loosely with plastic wrap or foil, and chill until completely cool, at least 30 minutes.

3. Meanwhile, combine bell pepper, green onions, mayonnaise, lemon juice, tarragon, white pepper, mustard powder, cayenne, and remaining ½ teaspoon salt in a large bowl; mix until combined.

4. Pull salmon from skin, and flake into bowl with bell pepper mixture. Gently mix until salmon is fully coated. (The salad should be chunky, not mushy.) Cover and chill at least 30 minutes and up to overnight.

5. To make the vinaigrette, in a small bowl, whisk together lemon juice, both oils, Dijon, sugar, and salt.

6. To prepare the rolls, place them on a baking sheet, and bake until warm, about 2 minutes. Slice open so they lay flat, but not all the way through. Brush insides with melted butter; return to oven and bake until lightly browned, 3 to 4 minutes.

7. Fill rolls with salmon salad, romaine, and tomatoes, and drizzle with vinaigrette.

Roosevelt Baked Beans

Yellowstone, which stretches from northwest Wyoming into Montana and Idaho, became the first national park in 1872. More than 150 years later, visitors stream into the park that launched it all to explore the thermal basin, hike, bike, snowmobile, or just relax. For an extra-special Yellowstone experience, sign up for the Old West Dinner Cookout at Wyoming's Roosevelt Lodge (open since 1920). You'll take a ride to an outdoor dining spot via horseback or covered wagon, then sit down for a steak dinner with all the sides, including the lodge's signature Roosevelt Baked Beans. What makes the dish so good? A base of ground beef and bacon; a sweet-savory brown sugar, vinegar, and mustard sauce; and four different kinds of beans.

YIELD: 8 TO 12 SERVINGS
HANDS-ON TIME: 10 MINUTES
TOTAL TIME: 1 HOUR 30 MINUTES

8 ounces ground beef or sausage

8 ounces bacon, finely diced

1 onion, finely chopped

1 (16-ounce) can pork and beans

1 (15-ounce) can kidney beans

1 (15-ounce) can lima beans

1 (15-ounce) can butter beans

½ cup packed brown sugar

½ cup ketchup

2 tablespoons apple cider vinegar

1 tablespoon spicy brown mustard

1 teaspoon garlic powder

Salt and pepper

1. In a large pot, cook beef and bacon over medium heat, stirring often, until beef is browned and bacon is crispy, about 15 minutes. Using a slotted spoon, transfer meat mixture to a plate. Pour off all but 1 tablespoon drippings from pot.

2. Add onion to pot with reserved drippings, and cook, stirring often, until softened, about 5 minutes. Stir in remaining ingredients.

3. Reduce heat to low, and simmer, stirring occasionally, until mixture thickens and flavors meld, about 1 hour. (You can also bake the beans at 325°F for about 45 minutes, if you prefer.)

Campfire Cobbler

Yellowstone's Roosevelt Lodge Cabins, which date back to 1920, are located in Wyoming and make the perfect home base for lots of adventures in the park. The rustic cabins (which don't have internet service) allow visitors to slow down and reconnect with nature, whether by relaxing in rocking chairs on the front porch and watching the birds fly by, saddling up for a horseback ride, or heading out to Pleasant Valley for the Old West Dinner Cookout. The popular outdoor meal ends with a skillet cobbler, which inspired the recipe here. Campfire coffee is an optional, but recommended, pairing.

YIELD: 8 SERVINGS
HANDS-ON TIME: 10 MINUTES
TOTAL TIME: 1 HOUR 10 MINUTES, INCLUDING COOLING

1¼ cups (150 grams) all-purpose flour

1 cup (200 grams) granulated sugar, divided

2 teaspoons baking powder

1 teaspoon ground cinnamon

½ teaspoon kosher salt

1 cup (240 milliliters) whole or 2% milk

1 teaspoon vanilla extract

¼ cup unsalted butter (½ stick), cut into cubes

4 cups fresh blueberries, raspberries, and blackberries

1 tablespoon lemon juice

1 teaspoon lemon zest

Heavy cream or vanilla ice cream, for serving

1. Preheat oven or grill to 375°F (aim for medium-high heat on a grill, 350°F to 400°F). In a medium bowl, whisk together flour, ¾ cup sugar, baking powder, cinnamon, and salt. Add milk and vanilla, stirring until just blended.

2. Place butter in a 10-inch cast-iron skillet. Place skillet in oven or on grill (covered with grill lid), and heat until butter is melted, about 5 minutes.

3. Meanwhile, in a medium bowl, toss berries with remaining ¼ cup sugar, lemon juice, and zest.

4. Carefully remove skillet from oven or grill, and swirl until bottom is coated with butter. Pour batter into skillet, and top with berry mixture.

5. Bake in oven or on grill (covered with grill lid) until golden brown and bubbling, 35 to 40 minutes. Let cool 10 minutes. Serve warm in bowls with either heavy cream or ice cream on top.

The dining room at Old Faithful Inn

Yosemite National Park

Burden baskets like the one shown here (1936) were used by Indigenous people to gather seeds, nuts, acorns, and bulbs from the landscape of Yosemite.

*Wassail (page 239) and Boysenberry Pie
(page 238)*

Boysenberry Pie

The premier lodge in California's Yosemite National Park—and perhaps across all the U.S. national parks—is the Ahwahnee, which originally opened in 1927. Its dining room, with its 34-foot-high ceilings, massive pine trestles, and granite pillars, is unrivaled. A longtime favorite on the menu is this pie made with boysenberries—a hybrid of different berries, including blackberries and raspberries. A slice, paired with a scoop of vanilla ice cream and views of the park from the floor-to-ceiling windows, is a sweet way to end the day in Yosemite.

YIELD: 8 SERVINGS
HANDS-ON TIME: 25 MINUTES
TOTAL TIME: 2 HOURS 15 MINUTES, INCLUDING CHILLING

CRUST

4 cups (480 grams) all-purpose flour

1 cup (2 sticks) plus 2 tablespoons unsalted butter, softened

3 tablespoons granulated sugar

3 ounces ice water

Pinch of salt

FILLING

1½ pounds frozen boysenberries or blackberries

¾ cup (150 grams) granulated sugar

1¼ ounces (5 tablespoons) instant clear gelatin (such as Instant Clearjel)

Pinch of salt

REMAINING INGREDIENTS

1 large egg, beaten

Coarse sugar, for sprinkling

1. To make the crust, in a food processor, combine flour, butter, sugar, water, and salt. Pulse until dough just comes together. Transfer to a clean surface, and form into 2 disks. Cover tightly with plastic wrap, and refrigerate for 1 hour or up to 2 days.

2. To make the filling, cook boysenberries in a medium saucepan over medium-low heat, stirring occasionally, for 5 minutes.

3. In a small bowl, whisk together sugar, gelatin, and salt. Stir into saucepan with berries. Cook, stirring frequently, for 5 minutes. Transfer to a bowl and cool slightly.

4. Preheat oven to 375°F. Roll out one dough disk, and fit into a 9- or 10-inch pie plate. Bake for 10 minutes. Transfer to a wire rack, and cool for 5 minutes.

5. Roll out remaining dough disk. Transfer berry mixture into cooled crust. Top with dough, crimping edges. Brush with egg, and sprinkle with coarse sugar. Cut a few small slits in top for steam to escape.

6. Bake pie until browned, 35 to 45 minutes, covering edges with foil or a pie shield if it starts browning too quickly. Cool completely before serving.

Wassail

Since it opened its doors in 1927, the Ahwahnee in California's Yosemite National Park has entertained presidents, royals, and other notable figures. The lodge's magnificent dining room is also known for exclusive events, and one of its biggest is the Bracebridge Dinner, held every December. The Yuletide celebration features a show—famed photographer Ansel Adams was one of the first cast members—and an extravagant dinner. While the menu has evolved over the years, some of the original dishes remain largely unchanged. One mainstay is the wassail, a warm cocktail that's sure to take the chill off a brisk Yosemite winter night.

YIELD: 8 TO 10 SERVINGS
HANDS-ON TIME: 20 MINUTES
TOTAL TIME: 1 HOUR 10 MINUTES

4 medium-size firm, sweet apples (such as Honeycrisp, Fuji, or Gala)

¼ cup packed brown sugar

¾ cup water

2 oranges, halved

12 whole cloves

1½ cups fresh or frozen cranberries

1 (2-inch) piece ginger, peeled and sliced

2 cinnamon sticks

½ gallon apple cider

1 individual bag hibiscus tea (optional)

1 cup ruby port, or cranberry or cherry juice

Garnishes: thinly sliced apples or oranges, cranberries, cinnamon sticks

1. Preheat oven to 350°F. Using a melon baller, scoop out cores from centers of apples (don't go all the way through the bottom, to help keep apples intact as they bake). Place apples, cored sides up, in a medium-size baking dish. Fill each with 1 tablespoon brown sugar. Pour ¾ cup water into bottom of baking dish, then bake until apples are tender but still have structure, 45 to 55 minutes.

2. Meanwhile, stud outsides of orange halves with 3 cloves each, and place, cut sides up, in a large Dutch oven or heavy-bottomed pot. Add cranberries, ginger, and cinnamon sticks. Pour apple cider over oranges and cranberries.

3. Bring to a boil over medium-high heat, then reduce heat to low, and simmer, covered, for 30 minutes. If using, add tea bag the last 10 minutes of simmering. Carefully strain mixture into a heatproof bowl, gently pressing with a spatula to release some of the liquid from fruit; discard strained solids.

4. Return strained liquid to pot. Stir in port. Transfer baked apples to pot, carefully tipping them on their sides to release the brown sugar. Gently stir. Serve wassail with desired garnishes.

Recipe Note

If not serving immediately, keep warm and covered either in pot over very low heat or in a slow cooker on warm. When the wassail is finished, the warm apples can be halved, served in bowls, and topped with ice cream for a decadent dessert. You can make this ahead for easier day-of serving; just gently reheat over medium heat.

Dirty Soda

Hiking, biking, backpacking, or birding among colorful sandstone cliffs attracts more than four million visitors to Utah's Zion National Park every year. Come summer, things heat up—with more visitors *and* higher temps. To cool off, reach for a dirty soda, a combination of soda (often Diet Coke), coconut creamer (or coconut syrup and half-and-half), and lime, which many say was invented by Swig Drinks, a Utah-based chain started in nearby St. George. Swing by Swig pre- or post-park, or pick up the ingredients for your cooler and have a DIY dirty soda whenever the mood strikes.

YIELD: 1 SERVING
HANDS-ON TIME: 5 MINUTES
TOTAL TIME: 5 MINUTES

Ice

1 (12-ounce) can cola soft drink (such as Diet Coke, Coca-Cola, or Dr Pepper)

2 tablespoons coconut-flavored coffee creamer

1 lime wedge, plus 1 lime wheel

1. Fill a tall glass with ice. Pour soda into glass, leaving about 1 inch at the top. Add creamer and juice from lime wedge (add more to taste, if desired). Garnish with lime wheel.

A canyon in the west of the park

Trail Mix Muffins

Investing in a good set of hiking boots is a must when heading to Zion, Utah's oldest national park. Stunning pink-and-red rock layers, some up to 270 million years old, are the park's main draw. Whether exploring these geologic masterpieces by hiking Angels Landing, climbing Mount Kinesava, or canyoneering the Subway, a pack full of fuel is also necessary. These hearty muffins—loaded with trail mix—are sure to get you through the day.

YIELD: 1 DOZEN MUFFINS

HANDS-ON TIME: 15 MINUTES

TOTAL TIME: 50 MINUTES, INCLUDING SOAKING AND COOLING

1 cup (90 grams) old-fashioned oats

1 cup (240 milliliters) dairy or nondairy milk

1 cup (120 grams) all-purpose flour

1 teaspoon baking powder

½ teaspoon baking soda

¼ teaspoon kosher salt

2 large eggs

¾ cup (165 grams) packed brown sugar

½ cup (1 stick) unsalted butter, melted and cooled

1½ teaspoons vanilla extract

1½ cups sweet trail mix, roughly chopped

1. In a medium bowl, stir together oats and milk. Let soak for 10 minutes.

2. Preheat oven to 375°F. Line a standard-size 12-cup muffin pan with paper liners, and lightly coat with cooking spray. In a large bowl, whisk together flour, baking powder, baking soda, and salt.

3. In another medium bowl, whisk eggs and sugar until thick and deep golden brown, about 2 minutes. Whisk in butter, vanilla, and oat-milk mixture.

4. Add wet ingredients to dry ingredients, stirring until blended. Stir in trail mix. Divide batter evenly among muffin cups. (The batter will nearly reach the tops of the cups.)

5. Bake until golden brown and a toothpick inserted into centers comes out clean, 18 to 20 minutes. Cool for 5 minutes, then transfer muffins to a wire rack to fully cool. Store muffins in a zip-top bag or an airtight container for up to 3 days, or freeze for up to 3 months.

Zion National Park

The Zion–Mount Carmel Highway (State Route 9) ushers visitors through millions of years of geologic history, past incredible landmarks like Checkerboard Mesa (shown here), and through the Zion–Mount Carmel Tunnel.

METRIC CONVERSION CHART

The recipes in this book were developed using standard U.S. measures following U.S. government guidelines. The charts below offer equivalents for U.S. and metric measures. All conversions are approximate and have been rounded up or down to the nearest whole number.

WEIGHT CONVERSIONS

ounces	grams
½	14
¾	21
1	28
1½	43
2	57
2½	71
3	85
3½	99
4	113
4½	128
5	142
6	170
7	198
8	227
9	255
10	283
12	340
16 (1 pound)	454

VOLUME CONVERSIONS

U.S.	metric
1 teaspoon	5 milliliters
2 teaspoons	10 milliliters
1 tablespoon	15 milliliters
2 tablespoons	30 milliliters
¼ cup	59 milliliters
⅓ cup	79 milliliters
½ cup	118 milliliters
¾ cup	177 milliliters
1 cup	240 milliliters
1¼ cups	296 milliliters
1½ cups	355 milliliters
2 cups (1 pint)	473 milliliters
2½ cups	591 milliliters
3 cups	710 milliliters
4 cups (1 quart)	0.946 liter
1.06 quarts	1 liter
4 quarts (1 gallon)	3.8 liters

OVEN CONVERSIONS

Fahrenheit	Celsius	gas mark
225	105	¼
250	120	½
275	135	1
300	150	2
325	165	3
350	180	4
375	190	5
400	200	6
425	220	7
450	230	8
475	245	9

ACKNOWLEDGMENTS

From Nina Elder

Allyson Johnson, our incredible editor, and I have tried to work together on a project for years. After many, many attempts (thank you for persisting!), the stars aligned with this book—and I couldn't be happier about that. Thanks to my parents (I love you, Mom and Dad!), I've loved the outdoors as long as I can remember and have spent some of my happiest moments exploring public lands. Pairing that passion with my love for food has been a dream come true.

This book would be nothing (truly) without my co-author, Melissa. Thank you for jumping in, taking charge, cooking your butt off, being endlessly patient and understanding, and sharing your immeasurable talents with me. I'm forever grateful and feel honored to share this book with you.

Finally, all the love and thanks and hugs to Matt and Gus, who were with me every step of the way during this project, as always. Your love and support is the reason I can do any of this. I love you. Let's celebrate with a walk in the woods!

From Melissa Knific

Just like a hike, the path through life is winding and can lead to some unexpected, beautiful moments. Publishing this cookbook is undoubtedly one of those, and it wouldn't have been possible if I hadn't met my co-author, Nina Elder, and my editor, Allyson Johnson, along the way.

I've been a Nina fan since we met nearly 15 years ago in a test kitchen. Nina, you have incredible food knowledge, thoughtful editing skills, and playful writing—not to mention you're poised and kind. Through you, I met Allyson and quickly recognized many of the same traits. I'm grateful to you both for bringing me into this project. It's been incredible to work with such smart, lovely, and supportive women.

Speaking of support, this moment also wouldn't exist without my family's cheerleading. Mom and Dad, your endless encouragement means everything to me. (Thank you, Mom, for the inspiration to pursue food as a career!) Eli, you gave me the courage to take the leap into freelance, and you've been my number one taste tester. Myles and Samara, you've helped me view life from a fresh perspective—that doing what I love makes me a better mom (and human). Thank you, family, for believing in me. I love you.

From Both of Us

We'd also like to thank Janet McCracken for her thoughtful and skillful recipe testing, Margo Rosenbaum for helping keep us organized and on track, Ashley Leath for her careful and thorough edits, and Becca Saltzman for seeing the recipes across the finish line.

And this book would just be words in a bunch of electronic documents if it weren't for the incredible photo and production crew. A huge thank you to the exceptional group of people who brought these recipes to life: photo editor Katie Dance, designer Jerry Sealy, creative director Elisa Gibson, director of photography Adrian Coakley, photographer Scott Suchman, food stylist Lisa Cherkasky, culinary producer Carolyn Robb, and digital technician Travis Marshall.

CREDITS

The food photographs on the cover and in the interior of this book were made by Scott Suchman, with food styling by Lisa Cherkasky and culinary production by Carolyn Robb.

Front cover (UP), Big Bend National Park, courtesy Lantern Press, (LO L to R) Hot Springs Smash Burger, Acadia Lobster Stew, Yellowstone Campfire Cobbler; back cover, (UP) Big Bend Entomatadas de Pollo, (LO L to R) Kenai Fjords Herb-Butter Halibut With Romesco, Everglades Mango-Passion-Banana Smoothie; 3, Elliot Hawkey; 4 (LO), DNY59/iStock/Getty Images; 6 (UP LE), Justin Reznick Photography/Moment/Getty Images; 6 (LO RT), Cliford Mervil; 7, Found Image Holdings/Corbis via Getty Images; 9, Graham Jepson/Alamy Stock Photo; 10-1 (map data), National Park Service; 12-3, NPS Photo; 14-5, Kelly Segré; 16-7, Xanterra Travel Collection; 18-9, Michael W. Harding; 20-1, The World Is A Book Travel Blog; 22-3, photo by Yang Song on Unsplash; 24 (UP), BW Folsom/Shutterstock; 24 (LO), Luc Rousseau/iStock/Getty Images; 26, Boston Public Library/Tichnor Brothers Postcard Collection; 28-9, University of Maine, Bert Call Collection; 32, Jonathan Irish; 34, Bryan Jolley/TandemStock; 35, Tom Grundy/Alamy Stock Photo; 40, Buddy Mays/Corbis Historical/Getty Images; 42, Bryan Schutmaat/National Geographic Image Collection; 48, from The New York Public Library; 50, Old New House; 52-3, Archive Photos/Getty Images; 54, Glenn Ruthven/Alamy Stock Photo; 60, Michael Nichols/National Geographic Image Collection; 64, kellyvandellen/iStock/Getty Images; 70, Ian Shive/TandemStock; 72, Oregon Historical Society, #bb000360; 78-9, Gene Lester/Archive Photos/Getty Images; 80, pho003228. L. F. Manis Photograph Collection. PH-00100. Special Collections and Archives, University Libraries, University of Nevada, Las Vegas. Las Vegas, Nevada; 82, NPS/Kurt Moses; 84, AlaskaPhotoGraphics/Patrick J Endres; 90, State Library and Archives of Florida via Florida Memory; 92-3, H. Armstrong Roberts/ClassicStock/Getty Images; 94, Erika Skogg; 98, Sean Pavone/Shutterstock; 102, NPS/Glacier National Park Archives; 105, Underwood Archives/Alamy Stock Photo; 108-9, Jim Heimann Collection/Archive Photos/Getty Images; 112, John Scott photo, Grand Canyon National Park Museum Collection, #GRCA 53492; 114, Katie Dance, NG; 117, Peter French/Design Pics; 118, Chris Burkard/Verb Photo; 120, Old New House; 124, Adam Mowery/TandemStock; 126, Jenny Adler/National Geographic Image Collection; 130-1, USGS Photo/D. Swanson; 134, Patrick Kelley/National Geographic Image Collection; 138, courtesy Eastern National; 140, Keith Ladzinski/National Geographic Image Collection; 142, Jonathan Irish; 144, William C. Alpin collection from the Los Angeles County Arboretum and Botanic Garden; 146, Keith Ladzinski; 150, HUM Images/Universal Images Group via Getty Images; 152-3, Michael Jones/Design Pics/Alamy Stock Photo; 155, Michael Jones/Design Pics; 156, Chris Burkard; 159, Katie Dance, NG; 160, AlaskaPhotoGraphics/Patrick J Endres; 162, Fred Hirschmann; 166, NPS/David Kem; 170, Shawn Mitchell Photo/Shutterstock; 178, Nathaniel Gonzales/Alamy Stock Photo; 182-3, Katie Dance, NG; 184, Elliot Hawkey; 194, Elliot Hawkey; 198, Katie Dance, NG; 203, Katie Dance, NG; 204-5, HUM Images/Universal Images Group via Getty Images; 206, Smith Collection/Gado/Getty Images; 208, Joel Mulbah; 212, NPS Photo; 214, Chuck Haney/DanitaDelimont/Alamy Stock Photo; 226, NPS Photo; 232, Katie Dance, NG; 234-5, NPS/Ralph H. Anderson; 240, H. Armstrong Roberts/ClassicStock/Getty Images; 244-5, Universal History Archive/Universal Images Group via Getty Images.

The recipes on the pages below were provided by the following restaurants, chefs, and contributors:

24, 26, Jordan Pond House; 30, Fresh Off Da Boat; 33, Milt's Stop & Eat; 38, 39, Reprinted from *The Sioux Chef's Indigenous Kitchen* by Sean Sherman with Beth Dooley. Published by the University of Minnesota Press, 2017. Copyright © 2017 Ghost Dancer, LLC. Used by permission of the author and the University of Minnesota Press; 60, Carlsbad Caverns Trading Company; 64, Mrs. Olson's; 70, Crater Lake Lodge; 76, 77, Ben Bebenroth; 80, The Oasis at Death Valley; 82, The Inn at Death Valley; 84, 86, Laura Cole; 88, Four Marlins restaurant; 112, El Tovar Hotel; 114, Signal Mountain Lodge; 117, Great Basin Cafe; 118, Oasis; 126, 127, Pipikaula and kudeesh sauce from *Cook Real Hawai'i: A Cookbook* by Sheldon Simeon with Garrett Snyder. Text copyright © 2021 by Sheldon Simeon. Used by permission of Clarkson Potter Publishers, an imprint of the Crown Publishing Group, a division of Penguin Random House LLC. All rights reserved; 128, Rosalinda Mariotti; 134, The Rim restaurant; 136, 138, Superior Bathhouse Brewery; 140, Fluid Coffee Roasters; 142, Rock Harbor Lodge and Lighthouse Restaurant; 144, Pappy & Harriet's restaurant; 155, Kenai Fjords Glacier Lodge; 156, 159, Kristine Kidd; 170, 172, Far View Lodge's Metate Room; 176, National Park Inn; 178, Tamarack Marketplace; 180, Lodge at Stehekin Restaurant; 188, 189, Painted Desert Diner; 192, Cocuyo's; 194, Moonstone Bar & Grill; 198, Bird & Jim; 206, Wuksachi Lodge's The Peaks Restaurant; 208, Skyland's Pollock Dining Room; 212, Theodore's Dining Room; 218, Morgan's Mango; 229, The Potato restaurant; 231, Roosevelt Lodge's Old West Dinner Cookout; 238, The Ahwahnee.

ABOUT THE AUTHORS

Nina Elder is an editor and writer with more than 20 years of experience. Although she's written about travel, health, kids' crafts, and more, the bulk of her career has focused on food. She's currently the deputy editor of food and drink at *Parade;* prior to that, she was the executive food director at The Kitchn, held multiple roles at Rachael Ray's magazines and *Bon Appétit,* and was a features editor at *Better Homes & Gardens.* She's passionate about snacks, well-written recipes, and having as much fun in the kitchen as possible. She lives in Rhode Island with her husband, son, and two rambunctious dogs, one of whom has a food-related name (Tater). Find her on Instagram @ninaelder.

Melissa Knific is an editor and recipe developer with a deep understanding of the home cook. She's a frequent contributor to the *New York Times* and TODAY Food. Formerly the food director of *Rachael Ray In Season,* a food editor at *Family Circle,* and a key member of HelloFresh's culinary team, she has created thousands of recipes for print and digital publishing and consumer products. She's also collaborated with Allrecipes, Simply Recipes, Delish, *Real Simple, Bon Appétit,* and, of course, National Geographic, where she most recently tested the entirety of *Big Moe's Big Book of BBQ* by pitmaster Moe Cason. She lives in New Jersey with her husband, two kids, and rescue dog. Find her at *melissaknific.com* or on Instagram @melissaknific.

Since 1888, the National Geographic Society has funded more than 15,000 research, conservation, education, technology, and storytelling projects around the world. National Geographic Partners distributes a portion of the funds it receives from your purchase to National Geographic Society to support their mission to illuminate and protect the wonder of our world.

National Geographic Partners, LLC
1145 17th Street NW
Washington, DC 20036-4688 USA

Get closer to National Geographic Explorers and photographers, and connect with our global community. Join us today at nationalgeographic.org/joinus

For rights or permissions inquiries, please contact
National Geographic Books Subsidiary Rights: bookrights@natgeo.com

Library of Congress Cataloging-in-Publication Data
Names: Elder, Nina author | Knific, Melissa author
Title: National Geographic national parks cookbook : dishes inspired by America's great outdoors / Nina Elder and Melissa Knific.
Description: Washington, D.C. : National Geographic Partners, LLC, [2025] | Includes index. | Summary: "Re-create iconic dishes found in your favorite national parks with this essential cookbook"-- Provided by publisher.
Identifiers: LCCN 2025012080 | ISBN 9781426224058 hardcover
Subjects: LCSH: Cooking, American | National parks and reserves--United States | LCGFT: Cookbooks
Classification: LCC TX715 .E383 2025 | DDC 641.5973--dc23/eng/20250327
LC record available at https://lccn.loc.gov/2025012080

The authorized representative in the EU for product safety and compliance is
Disney Trading B.V., Asterweg 15S, 1031 HL, Amsterdam, The Netherlands
email: DCP.DL-EU.bookscontact@disney.com

Printed in China

25/RRDH/1

EXPLORE THE WILD
WITH THE NATIONAL PARK EXPERTS

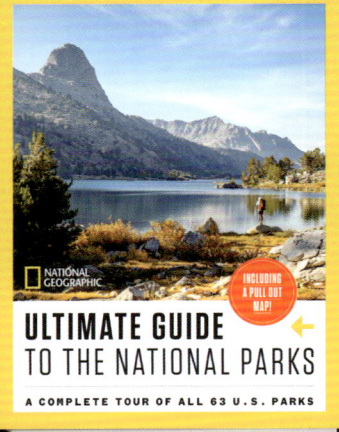

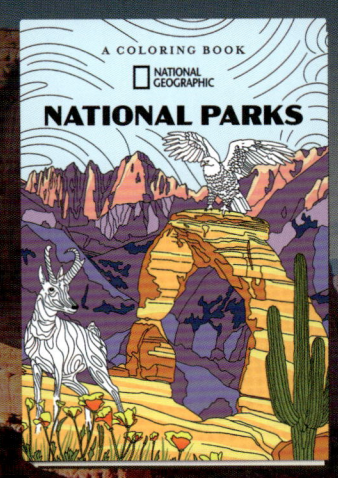

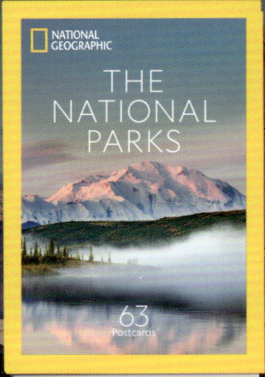

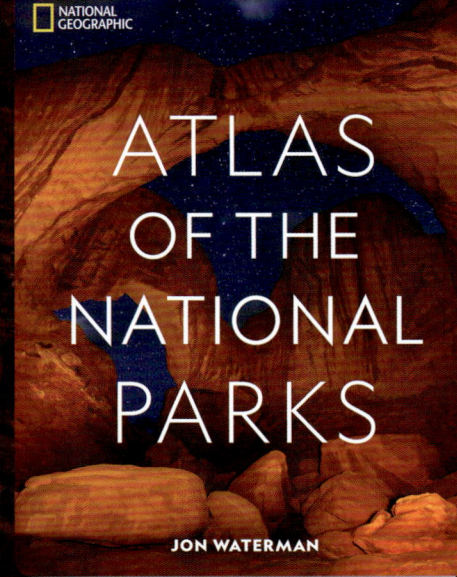

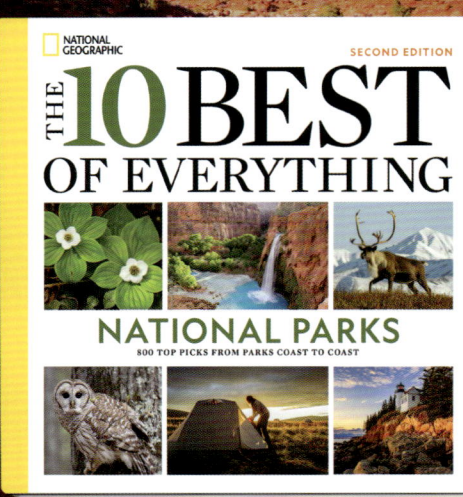